"Do not miss these Wesleyan churc
'originality' is: a return flip to origin., ...
and fresh out" of the first and original."

M000010042

—Leonard Sweet
best-selling author, professor (Drew University, Tabor College,
George Fox University), and architect / chief contributor
to preachthestory.com

"After reading *Flipping Church*, I'm increasingly hopeful about the
future of our denomination! The church needs hopeful inspiration
like this from the 'permissionaries on the bleeding edges' of church
and innovation."

—Rev. Amy Barker Valdez, PhD
Executive Secretary, United Methodist Connectional Table

"This is a must-read for anyone who longs to see the church thrive in the
Twenty-first Century. Each chapter gives voice to a unique perspective
and context of faith community development that is honest, heartfelt,
wise, and hopeful. What a delight to sit at the feet of these apostles as
they share their stories of discerning God's call and vision for that new
thing that longs to spring forth. They share glimpses of what it means
to innovate, experience failure, and prevail in grace-filled ways."

—Beth Ann Estock and **Paul Nixon**
coauthors of *Weird Church: Welcome to the Twenty-First Century*

"*Flipping Church* brings together stories from a variety of labors of
love by passionate church planters. The book calls the church to offer
Christ in new and meaningful ways in making the gospel real to the
post-Christian world. Prophetic, pastoral, missional, and insightful,
the book will help readers understand the dynamics of new forms
of being the church that God is creating. Church hierarchy, and both
lay and clergy leaders, will benefit from its insights into the nature of
leadership needed for this new mission field into which God is calling
us to venture. It is absolutely fascinating to read stories of the fruits
of a risk-taking ministry undertaken by modern-day church planters
with Wesleyan DNA. It is an inspiring, challenging, and empowering
book for those who want to start new faith communities and for existing churches who desire to better understand our world."

—Sudarshana Devadhar
Resident Bishop, New England Annual Conference

"*Texas Methodist Foundation* is committed to providing financial and leadership resources for a new generation of entrepreneurial church planters who are turning the traditional notions of church planting upside-down. These gifted new leaders see unexpected places and ways where God is working and then create life-transforming, world-changing opportunities for accomplishing God's dreams for this world. In this remarkable book, Michael Baughman and his fellow church planting adventurers share a wonderful variety of new learnings that are must-reading for those of us who want to join with them in God's 'new thing.'"

—Tom Locke
President, Texas Methodist Foundation

"From the apostle Paul to John Wesley, Christian history is filled with brave, revolutionary souls who felt the Spirit moving them to new lands and the communities that gathered around them. Thankfully, Twenty-first-Century United Methodism has its own pioneers who have felt called beyond the familiar terrain of established pulpits. Their compiled stories tell of the steep challenges and deep blessings they discovered while planting faith communities amid various cultural, geographic, and economic settings. Diverse in experiences, gifts, and methods, their collective testimony reminds us that the Holy Spirit is still moving in mighty ways, that the church prevails in all shapes and sizes, and that apostles called to roads less traveled are not alone. Whether you are a pastor seeking inspiration, a church planter seeking wisdom, or a disciple seeking hope, this book is for you."

—Rev. Beth Ludlum
Vice President for Strategic Initiatives,
Wesley Theological Seminary

"If you are interested in the changing contours of ministry in the Twenty-first Century, *Flipping Church* is a must-read. Mike Baughman and his collaborators deliver spirited hope for the future with a hopeful spirit for today!"

—Jim Ozier
coauthor of *Clip In* and *The Changeover Zone*

"*Flipping Church* offers a hopeful riposte to the incessant shouting that the church is dying or already dead. Following the likes of butterflies and the empty tomb, Baughman and his team of writers remind us that God has a way of bringing new and beautiful life to what we thought was gone forever. I dare you to read this book and not well up with gratitude for their collective work and God's faithfulness to the church.

—**Nate Phillips**
author of *Do Something Else: The Road Ahead for the Mainline Church*

"One of Steve Jobs's business rules was to never be afraid of cannibalizing yourself. 'If you don't cannibalize yourself, someone else will,' he said. So even though an iPhone might cannibalize the sales of an iPod, or an iPad might cannibalize the sales of a laptop, that did not deter him.

We live in a United Methodist world that often is so afraid of cannibalizing itself that we fear innovation. We have overbuilt buildings and in our attempts to keep them full, we have failed to innovate, which only helps us to fail faster in a new day.

Baughman and his colleagues boldly march us off the map, opening up their R&D notebooks for us to get a glimpse into the creative process in all its messiness. From the outset they tell us these are not prescriptions but rich descriptions of what can be.

As we walked through the cemetery across from Wesley's City Road Chapel in London recently, a colleague remarked to me, 'If we did today, the kind of things Wesley did back then, we would lose our credentials.' This book testifies that we can follow in Wesley's footsteps without losing our credentials while regaining our credibility with the communities in which we are planting new places."

—**Phil Schroeder**
Director of Congregational Development,
North Georgia Annual Conference

FLIPPING
CHпRCH

How Successful Church Planters Are Turning Conventional Wisdom Upside-Down

EDITED BY

MICHAEL BAUGHMAN

DISCIPLESHIP
RESOURCES

ISBNs
978-0-88177-853-3 (print)
978-0-88177-854-0 (mobi)
978-0-88177-855-7 (ePub)

Library of Congress Control Number: 2016911718

DR853

CONTENTS

PREFACE

In the summer of 2013, the staff of Path 1 (New Church Starts at Discipleship Ministries of The United Methodist Church) along with a selected group of associates from around the United States embarked on an extensive road trip during which we visited more than 320 of the new churches that were planted in the previous five years. Through hundreds of conversations with church planters and judicatory leaders of congregational development, we learned about the hopes and heartaches of starting new places for new people and revitalizing existing churches among the people called Methodist in the United States. We learned of innovative out-of-the-box church plants as well as traditional strategies that are reaching new people and making disciples of Jesus Christ for the transformation of the world. We celebrated the many ways that annual conferences and districts of the church are finding ways to form new communities of faith. We also learned that there was a lack of resources to guide new church planting in a Wesleyan theological perspective. As a result, we set out to create Wesleyan Church Planting Resources. Our hope is that these resources will not only help those who plant new churches but also help in the revitalization of existing churches.

Flipping Church is the second book to be published as part of this initiative. Michael Baughman, an innovative church planter in Dallas, Texas, had the vision of bringing together a group of church planters to write about the various ways in which new church planting is turning upside down traditional notions of how to be the church. I know that you will learn about new approaches to ministry by reading this book, and I know that it will not only help endeavors to start new places for new people but also stimulate conversation for existing churches as they seek to reach people in their communities.

Douglas Ruffle
General Editor of Wesleyan Church Planting Resources

Other Titles in Path1's Wesleyan Church Planting Resources Series

Vital Merger, by Dirk Elliott (foreword by Douglas T. Anderson); Fun & Done Press, 2013

A Missionary Mindset: What Church Leaders Need to Know to Reach Their Community—Lessons from E. Stanley Jones, by Douglas Ruffle; Discipleship Resources, 2016

FOREWORD: CARTOGRAPHERS

KENDA CREASY DEAN AND MARK DEVRIES
MINISTRY INCUBATORS, INC

You hold in your hands one of the first scouting reports of the cartographers of the church of the future. The women and men you will meet in these pages are pioneers, mapping uncharted territory and forging new congregational life-forms. What may one day be obvious and "normal" for congregations fifty years from now may seem strange and foreign to the average early twenty-first century church lover.

To make a map is less an act of mathematical precision than a way to tell a story.[1] Early cosmologists drew the universe with the earth at its center; medieval cartographers made detailed drawings of the world they knew, and simply left blank unexplored expanses (someone later annotated one of these maps with the warning, "Here be dragons"). Storytellers know the value of a map: Robert Louis Stevenson's *Treasure Island* sprang from a map painted by his twelve-year-old stepson; A. A. Milne sketched the Hundred Acre Wood; before drafting the Lord of the Rings trilogy, J. R. R. Tolkien (who had charted enemy trenches during World War I) doodled a map of Middle-Earth on an examination paper at Oxford and spent years revising it, gluing successive versions on top of former ones. "If you're going to have a complicated story," Tolkien explained, "you must work to a map; otherwise you'll never make a map of it afterwards."[2]

The twenty-first century church is nothing if not a complicated story, and church leaders—like mapmakers and storytellers—must try to make sense of this world for those who come after us. The church planters in this volume have stories to tell. Like cartographers, they all draw their landscapes with the colors of their own biases, assumptions, and experiences. They do not prescribe as much as demonstrate how they have judged their cultural terrain and responded to it as a mission field that God has already embraced.

This last point is crucial. Thankfully, this is not a generation of missionaries who believe they are responsible for God's travel plans. They don't think of themselves as bringing Jesus to people who lack him. They view themselves as explorers and discoverers, people on the lookout for where God is already at work in neighborhoods and in people who may or may not have had anything to do with churches. As pastors, they dust the scene for divine fingerprints that point to the fact that Christ has already been there and point out pockets of resurrection wherever they exist.

Of course, they (and we) don't always get it right. Like all good adventurers, church planters see possibilities for Christian community that are not obvious to the rest of us, and not all of these ideas will stand the test of time. Yet the bold creativity reflected in these pages—and the sheer courage of those willing to turn "normal church" on its ear for the sake of the gospel—inspires us, and we're willing to bet it inspires you too. Heaven knows, the church needs pioneers right about now. Perhaps you are called to be one of them.

Pioneers are not a terribly efficient lot. Instead of taking the well-worn path where progress (or at least the illusion of progress) is rapid and rewards are clear, they head for the road less travelled, following bread crumbs more often than pavement because they are convinced that God lives among the weeds as well as along the highway. Few obstacles stand in the way of church leaders who want to form yet one more committee; this can be easily done. But too often, the well-worn path simply circles around the altar to "the way we've always done it around here."

In this book you won't meet many committee creators. Instead, you will encounter inefficient pioneers, people who are still whacking their way through the brush as they cut their own path toward the future church. It's a much slower journey, to be sure, than replicating the present, and it's a hike without an absolutely certain destination. Some of these paths will lead to dead ends, but a few, maybe a precious few, will usher us into an undiscovered expanse for ministry.

Having spent so much of our lives in the world of youth ministry, the *de facto* research and development department of the church, we have a deep affinity for creativity and for the need for innovation to go mainstream in Christian communities. Young adults in our time have little patience for the tedium of what a Southern pastor friend of mine refers to as "chicken-eatin'-do-nothin'-meetings." They are weary of churches battling passionately (more often than not, against each other) over all the wrong things. They have had enough of churches that spend the vast majority of their energy and resources on survival and self-promotion.

Okay, let's be frank. It's not just young people. We feel the same way.

In the organizational life cycle, there are those on the leading edge and those on the "bleeding edge." The latter are so far ahead of their time that they will face steep resistance, leaving them bloody and limping from their foray into innovation. The former, the leading edge folks, are the ones who come just behind the bleeding edge, those who take radical ideas and turn them into a widely embraced new normal. We are unspeakably grateful to Mike Baughman for rounding up both kinds of characters and enterprises for this book (and for being a bleeding/leading edge character himself).

There is little doubt that, two or three decades from now, the church as we know it will be a very different place. With shrinking resources, most will no longer have the luxury of standing still. Most will be required to either innovate or die. We think that is great news for the church, because it forces us to take a good hard look at who Christ calls us to be and navigate to that point, whether we have maps to guide us or not. Let's go even further: we happen to think this is the best opening for ministry that most churches have had in a few centuries. We can take nothing about our current church organizations for granted; we can assume that no future we have imagined so far accurately depicts the future God has in store for us. This is the grand adventure of ministry: to hold tight to Christ and follow wherever the Spirit leads—which, we can be sure, is a journey that won't end where we already are.

Kenda Creasy Dean and Mark DeVries

Kenda Creasy Dean and **Mark DeVries** are the cofounders and chief permissionaries for Ministry Incubators, Inc. (ministryincubators.com), an incubator program and consulting group for early-stage missional entrepreneurs. When not teaching at Princeton Theological Seminary or leading *Youth Ministry Architects*, they invest their time and experience in individuals, organizations, and faith communities who want to turn harebrained ideas for ministry into sustainable missional enterprises.

INTRODUCTION

A New Old-Fashioned Way to Be Wesleyan

MICHAEL BAUGHMAN, EDITOR

St. Paul's Cathedral dominates much of London's skyline. Her great dome displays the splendor of mother church, adorned in gold. Supported by stone and financial endowment, the mighty church building will stand as long as London stands. The edge of the cathedral grounds presents a statue of John Wesley. Facing the church, his hands and feet make a statement. His left hand clutches a Bible close to his heart. His right hand points to heaven, the power of God behind the edifice before him. A few feet from Wesley's statue opens a gate to the city of London. What strikes me most about Wesley's story, captured in this silent statue, are his feet. Wesley is clearly on the move, offering a reminder of our purpose to the church before he walks through the gate to the city he loved. This is the proper place for Wesley in the city of London. No cold statue of Wesley's dead body lies in church repose. He is on the grounds of a church he never left, but right at the gate. His feet tread the thin space between church and culture, powerful and needy, sacred and secular.

This is the same space that authors in this book occupy. They remain in the church that formed them, but few are constructing cathedrals or resting in the protective structures built by those who have gone before. Fewer still are worshipping in school cafetoriums with rented supplies from church-in-a-box. Don't get me wrong: we need pastors in cafetoriums establishing new ministries at the edge of suburban development. The entrepreneurial pastors in this book, however, occupy a different space. They are the vanguard of a growing regiment of Methodists who break new ground. Their witness reminds us that being "Wesleyan" has as much to do with their creative drive as it does any particular theology.

Wesleyan Creativity

The more I get to know the story of the early Methodists, the more I realize that Wesleyan character should be defined as much by a willingness to innovate as anything else. When John Wesley moved his ministry to Bristol, he willingly became "vile" for the sake of the gospel and preached in places he did not want to go. When Wesley, Whitfield, and others "preached before thousands" in town squares and country fields, those passing on the way home from work were counted just as much as one who showed up in a tabernacle or meeting hall. While some of that work may be the eighteenth-century version of inflated preacher numbers, it allowed the early movement to connect with those who would never darken the doors of a church—save to get married or baptized.

This innovative spirit permeated Methodist work in less obvious ways as well. Class, band, and society meetings were innovative means to not just create small group accountability but also spread messages and mobilize people for action. In essence, while inventing small groups, the early Methodists created their own social media. Before there was amazon.com, John Wesley was stuffing the saddlebags of circuit riders with books to sell—simultaneously supporting the movement financially while spreading

it literally. In so doing, early Methodists invented and executed
an early form of social enterprise as an alternative way to sustain the work of the church. They developed creative means to
train pastors, give them rest, and send them out from specially
designed quarters in Bristol. The early Methodists utilized technology, print media, and music in a way that the Church of England would take decades to adopt. Innovation seeped into the very
places they rested their butts. Meeting rooms and worship spaces
were furnished with adjustable-back benches rather than pews.
With a simple movement, the back moved to the other side of the
bench so that people could turn and face those behind them. This
allowed for conversation and small groups after hearing from a
preacher or teacher. Innovation made the Methodist movement a
reality and injected enthusiasm for God's ongoing creative work.

While entrenched factions in the church argue whether it is
more Wesleyan to fight for justice or evangelize (spoiler: it's both),
the pioneer legacy of Methodism and witness from the pages of
this book insist that being Wesleyan is as much about a way of
ministry as it is any particular theology. The planters contributing
to this book favor innovation over convention and creativity over
comfort. Each of these planters breaks some rule of conventional
church wisdom in order to care for their distinct neighborhood
and setting. They inspire me to be a better pastor, a braver disciple, and a louder champion for their cause. My hope is that this
book will inspire you to innovate within your own context, break
routine, and escape "business as usual." I would not encourage
every reader to break all of the wisdom questioned by all twelve
contributors. None of the authors in this book adopted new means
of ministry lightly. They did so in order to meet the particular
needs of their context and calling. More than tips or tricks on how
to start a new church, they offer a "permissionary" witness to
those who want to venture out with their congregation and neighborhood to the leading edge.

The Cost and Call of Creativity

All of the authors in this book have experimented boldly. All of them have failed along the way. We ought not seek failure, but we must remember it is part of the price for innovation. On the one hand, I hope that from these pages you will garner ideas that may be helpful for your work in service to God. On the other, far more important hand, I hope that in these pages you will find the permission to breathe a bit more deeply of God's innovative spirit. We, as Methodists, are in a far better position to dream, risk, imagine, and experiment than denominational doomsday cries would suggest. We are one of the most property-rich organizations in the United State of America. We are steepled with endowments. Unlike smaller religious organizations with fewer resources and people, we can afford to fail brilliantly and repeatedly in order to find creative paths to the future church. We can lose on one thousand gambles if it helps us find the one new solution that carries us on to the next great era of church, but we will never fly if we just put yellow caution tape around the cliffs that surround us.

Cutting-edge church planting is not just Wesleyan, it's divine. The first commandment that God gives to humanity in Genesis 1:28 is to "be fruitful and multiply." This is not just an invitation but a command to participate in the great, creative work of God. At this point in the biblical story, the only thing we know God as is Creator. As soon as God creates humanity, the divine work is shared with us! The opportunity to create that which did not previously exist is nothing short of divine!

Despite this reality, churches have a tendency to weed out entrepreneurial pastors. These clergy generally make us uncomfortable because creation is difficult to control. (Just ask God about certain circumstances that led to a rather large boat in Genesis 6.) To create something new is to risk more than just failure—that which we create may grow out of our control or the comfort zones of the powers that be. Indeed, this was the concern voiced by many in the Church of England about Wesley's work. To be fair, history reveals that if institutional stability and unity were of highest priority, then many of Wesley's critics were right. Today the worldwide Methodist movements stand apart as unplanned pregnancies off of the Anglican Communion. We have loose official ties, at best, to our mother church. Viewed from another perspective, the Methodist movement allowed much of the Church of England to continue ministry in a place (the Americas) where social and political realities prohibited the Church of England from standing as a beacon for Jesus Christ. Methodist innovation—even to a point of standing apart from the mother denomination—allowed an Anglican legacy to continue.

This book only highlights twelve bold Methodist church planters who have found some measure of success (an elusive term) and offer lessons to the church. There are far more innovative pastors out there and far more still who took a leap of faith and crashed to the ground. Their work is no less valuable. Their lessons inform those who come after. Failure and mistakes are the cost of innovation. It might benefit our annual conferences to celebrate and learn from church plants that did not become sustainable. It may benefit us to hear their stories—what worked and what they couldn't quite get right—in the hope that those who follow might be able to build upon their work. I believe I speak for all the authors in this book when I express gratitude for the bravery, tenacity, and inspiration of those who have gone before us.

Chasing a Creative Wesleyan Spirit

As you read through this book, you will see similar trends and perspectives from one chapter to the next. Though not uniform, these consistencies are telling of deeper work being done by the Holy Spirit across diverse ministry settings. It is our duty and our joy as Wesleyans to follow this Holy Spirit work. This is the same spirit that swept across the waters and brought forth life, the same spirit that gave breath to an army of Israelite corpses, the same spirit that inspired John Wesley to reform the nation and spread scriptural holiness throughout the land. This is the God who says "Behold, I AM making all things new." The church is not excluded from this great prophecy. Behold, the great I AM is making things new through the work of the authors in this book and church leaders like you. May we follow Wesley's witness, stand in that thin space between the church and the rest of the world, and be blessed for our efforts.

Start a Church. Bring God to the Neighborhood.

MICHAEL BAUGHMAN, UNION COFFEE

You have heard it said . . .

"Offer them Christ." Thomas Coke was a young pastor, recently ordained, heading off to America to organize a Methodist movement in the wake of political revolution. As Coke's boat slid away from the harbor, the classic story says that John Wesley shouted one last time, "Offer them Christ!"

Before my grandfather was a pastor in the Evangelical Church, he was a preacher's kid, entertaining himself with toy airplanes during sermons. He occasionally interrupted worship with the sounds of airborne acrobatics and imagined machinegun fire. When his mother died tragically young, the love of Christ comforted my grandfather. As difficult family decisions had to be made, he called upon their faith to guide his ethics and give him confidence in the murk swirled up by emotions, heartache, and an imperfect world. When his and my great grandfather's denomination

---

Michael Baughman is the Community Curator and Founding Pastor for Union Coffee in Dallas, Texas. ◆ uniondallas.org

7

merged with another to form the Evangelical United Brethren and eventually another to form the United Methodist Church, he knew that Christ is what mattered most and continued in ministry. Throughout his life, "offer them Christ" guided my grandfather. Offer them the same hope, comfort, forgiveness, purpose, life that God has given to you. He was a missionary to Japan. He planted churches from Pennsylvania to Alaska. He dedicated his life to offering Christ.

I am proud to follow in my grandfather's footsteps as a church planter. I'm a third-generation Methodist minister who married a sixth-generation Methodist minister. Wesley, it seems, is in my blood. And yet, I find myself planting a church in a very different way from my grandfather. Although I have opened a coffee shop, named Union, as a site for ministry, conversation, worship, and discipleship, the fact that we serve coffee is not what most sets me apart from many of my evangelical, Calvinist friends or even from my deeply rooted, Wesleyan grandfather. While "offer them Christ" has been helpful to my grandfather and many other missionaries in the world, I find myself latching onto another element of Wesley's charge.

A year after graduating from seminary, I fell in love with a Texan and moved to a state I never thought I would see, let alone live in. I think I saw myself as a bit of a missionary to Fort Worth, Texas, bearing with me the glittering, enlightened culture of an ivy-league educated, liberal Yankee. I wouldn't just be an amazing minister. They already had Christ. I would offer them enlightenment!

It didn't go well.

The first time I sat down in the office of my district superintendent he said to me, "Mike, you've got to realize that you've got three strikes against you walking in this door." He wasn't joking. "You're from New Jersey, you went to Duke, and you went to Princeton.

That's going to be a lot for people to overcome." I lacked grace. I lacked roots. I lacked cultural awareness. Some people only saw what I lacked.

> **Hall:** In that context, you were, like the apostle Paul, "one untimely born . . . the least of all the apostles and not even deserving to be called an apostle" (1 Corinthians 15:8-9). But God is happy to use those kinds of people!

So much for the ivy-league educated, liberal Yankee.

Others saw past my ill-conceived sense of self and purpose. They saw past what I lacked to what God was doing through me, in spite of me. They loved and nurtured those parts of me that were best. They were never coercive. They even wanted to learn from me when they had so much to teach.

Through them, I learned a new way of leadership and a new way of evangelism. "Offer them Christ" sees what someone lacks and offers it to them. It establishes an imbalanced power dynamic that sets the object of mission beneath the planter. Through those who believed in God's work through me, I learned how to minister in a wholly or perhaps holy different way.

But I say to you . . .

Although Jesus is at the heart of what we do at Union Coffee, "offer them Christ" is not our guiding principle. We did not plant our church to bring God to the neighborhood or Jesus into the lives of those who walk in our doors. We believe that God is already at work in our neighborhood, that Jesus is already at work in the lives of the people who walk in our doors. Our responsibility is to see what God is doing in our neighborhood and become a part of that.

> **Hall:** I love this. A leader at my church recently gave a testimony about how church had given her a new pair of glasses through which to see herself, the church, and the world. I *do* think that a growing percentage of people who have no formation or experience of faith or spiritual reality will need a sensitive but robust "catechesis" through which they actually might experience feeling Christ offered to them. But I love what you're saying: that the pastoral work is not about inserting some truth which isn't there (though cognitive and intellectual teaching is surely part of discipleship) but helping people see the existential truth which has always been there, in them, running through them, but which they had not yet become aware of.

This perspective does not come from Eastern philosophy or generic good feelings. It comes from our Wesleyan heritage.

Throughout Wesley's life, he heavily emphasized the presence of God and what a gift it is. This contributed to his emphasis on practices like Communion and shaped his deathbed words when he focused not on justifying grace but instead declared, "The best of all is that God is with us." Better than all the many things he had preached on, lived, hoped for, and done—his final confidence was placed in the presence of God.

He wrote extensively about this presence and its significance before his deathbed. In 1788 he penned Sermon 111, "On the Omnipresence of God." In it, I found two questions that, more than anything, have shaped Union's approach to church planting.

> What shall we make of this awful consideration [that God is present in all things]? . . . Should we not labour continually to acknowledge his presence? (III.1)

What Shall We Do

When developing the concept for Union, we struggled with the admonition to "offer them Christ" and the typical planting mentality, because it is laden with assumptions that we wished to avoid:

1. "We" (holy types) are distinct from "they" (our neighbors, who are not as "Jesus-y" as we are).
2. We possess divine knowledge (something we hold with the greatest value) that others do not have. This creates an implied hierarchy that makes it difficult to be in ministry with young people—especially those burned by the church.
3. Our neighborhoods are "mission fields." No one wants to be considered a part of someone else's mission field, but people are happy to be in a "neighborhood."
4. God is somehow more present in "sacred" places and people, and somehow less present in "secular" places and people.

Hall: This is, thanks be to God, an idea that is much more mainstream these days, perhaps owing to the conversation around nondualism. I'm interested in how congregations might actually practice this idea as a *community*. You'll often hear people talk about experiencing God while on a hike, watching the sunset, and so forth, which is glorious and all well and good, but they're often describing an individual moment. What would it look like for the church to, together as a community, be out in "secular" places, looking for God, and testifying to the presence of God in that context? What if a central part of Christian discipleship were learning to be public about faith: to regularly experience what it's like to be consciously present in the world, asking people questions, listening to people, and responding to them in contextually sensitive ways? At my church, we regularly commission people to stand at mass transit stations, walk in parades, sponsor booths at farmer's markets, and the like so that they can practice this secular-sacred coherence.

Church planting rooted in the omnipresence of God shifts the standard church planting perspective in subtle ways that significantly transform the community and the church. Our responsibility as the church isn't to necessarily change the lives of individuals or our community. That is God's work. Our responsibility, instead, is to set our imagination loose, open wide our ears, listen for the easily overlooked symphony of God that plays in the broken corners of our neighborhood, and join in on God's great work. I have consistently found that when I look for God, I'm rarely disappointed and always inspired.

Sorority Girls and Jocks

For far too long, the church has believed that because we are in the business of God, we somehow have a monopoly on best practices and the divine. When I read the New Testament, however, I see a rambunctious Jesus who rejects conformity to the categories we use to describe him. The reality is that God will never be confined by our structures and standards. I believe our distinctions between "sacred" and "secular" mean little to God. If Jesus, then, is at work outside of the church as well as inside it, the church can learn much about community, discipleship, and God from the world around us.

A lot of sorority girls study at Union. In our first couple months of operations, I had gotten to know several leaders from the local Delta Delta Delta (tri-delt) chapter. I invited a few of them to a Friday-evening event Union was having in mid-January, and they laughed. "Rush begins that Monday, so we can't do anything on Friday night." Seeing the puzzled look on my face, one explained, "We have to memorize the names of all the girls who are going through rush."

"That's hundreds of girls," I replied. They shrugged. "So you spend the whole weekend memorizing their names?" I asked.

She looked around, as if to see if anyone was listening, and then leaned in closer to me. "Do you think it's an accident that every girl who rushes tri-Delt feels like they fit in? We have a plan for every person who walks through our doors."

"What do you mean?" I asked, intrigued.

"Let's say a girl comes up to our door. We don't look at her name tag but greet her by name nonetheless. She's introduced to someone who is from the same town as her. Then she's introduced to someone who played the same sport in high school, and then she's connected with someone who has the same major as her. Everyone feels welcome. Everyone has something to talk about with the women they meet. And that's just the beginning."

I leaned back in my chair and realized that if churches spent one-tenth the time on evangelism and hospitality that the average American sorority spends, churches might retain visitors at a much higher rate. Nobody is talking about the decline of sororities in America.

Hall: I totally agree. Why has "let people find their own way" become the standard operating procedure in many of our churches? For most people, and particularly people new to faith community exploration, an intimate, focused approach is helpful. We need for a discipleship "system" that includes (a) on-ramps/ entry points for different kinds of people at different "levels" of spiritual/faith development; (b) clear, intentional pathways that address the question "tell me in some detail what I need to do to grow?"/ "what are the steps from where I am to the next leg of the journey?" (program pieces might be small groups, service projects, etc.—discipleship is the integration of all these orbs); and (c) a system for close tracking of folks moving along this journey, from first time guest to committed member. How are folks followed up with?

We don't have any biker gangs at Union, but we do have a moped gang. The men and women who run Crossfit North Central come to Union for all of their staff meetings, so a half-dozen buff athletes regularly pull up on their mopeds. As I've had conversations with them, I've learned why people are so devoted to Crossfit. They clearly articulate what sets it apart from other fitness programs, offer measurable results, and build a community that cares for each other in and out of the gym. I know a lot of people who will miss church on a Sunday morning when something else comes up. I don't know a lot of Crossfitters who will miss their regular workout when other opportunities present themselves. Crossfit knows more about membership than, I think, most churches do.

When Union developed a membership preparation process, we asked sorority girls, along with some people who run a Crossfit gym, to help us design our membership system. It's a five-month process, and two years in, it's one of the best things we have going for us. That sorority girl that I first talked to, Carissa, has not only become a part of our worshipping community but now leads the team that plans a new worship service on Sunday nights for young professionals and the Dallas arts community. We saw what God was doing in her life, asked her to apply her skills at Union, and in the process have all had the opportunity to encounter God in powerful ways.

Changing the World One Cape at a Time

Cody's tattoos and facial hair make him look kind of like a pirate. He would study at Union with a group of attractive young women. (As a male nursing student, the odds were in his favor.) Cody was not interested in the church. He had left, burned. When I talked with him about our Tuesday night worship gathering, he was not

interested and avoided Union on Tuesday nights for a year. Still, we built a solid friendship.

He forgot, one Tuesday, about our worship gathering when he needed to study for his comprehensive exams. Surrounded by a community at worship, he studied with headphones on, but I saw his mouth move with the words to a couple of the songs. A week later, he was studying at Union and didn't put his earphones on. I asked him if he wanted to grab lunch.

While meeting, he told me about an idea that he and another recent graduate, Jordan, had. They wanted to make capes for the children they had met in their pediatrics rotation, dress up like heroes, and empower the kids with capes. They were able to make some but quickly ran out of money and volunteers. They didn't have a lot of sewing expertise either. The idea never developed the way he had dreamed.

Union has a lot of donors who care about kids. Two sewing groups meet at Union, and we're connected to church sewing groups. We have access to a long list of volunteers.

Cody, Jordan, a couple of key volunteers, and I began work on a new initiative, Capes 4 Kids. Once a month, we turn our coffee shop into a cape-making factory and crank out as many kid-sized capes as we can. Then a team of volunteers dresses up like superheroes and delivers the capes to children with chronic illnesses in the Dallas area. In one year, we produced over five hundred capes. Each cape says, "Powered by Union and the United Methodist Church."

Wouldn't it be great if the United Methodist Church were known as the people who put capes on the backs of children with chronic illnesses? Four churches across the country have joined us in Capes 4 Kids. We hope that many more will too. All of this is possible because we assumed God was at work in the lives of people who walked in our doors.

Cody *and* Jordan (who was not attending a church) started coming to worship on a regular basis. They also bring their friends.
Cody serves on the team that now plans our worship gatherings,
and Jordan is a constant presence in our ministries, constantly
offering her time to support the work of Jesus Christ.

Live and Move and Have Our Being

Church planting rooted in the omnipresence of God was not
invented by Union or John Wesley. It's a biblical concept dem-
onstrated most clearly by Paul when he traveled to Athens (Acts
17:16-34)—a cosmopolitan, multiethnic, and multireligious city
like Dallas, our city for ministry. When Paul arrives in Athens,
he is distressed by the many idols he sees. We might assume he
begins his ministry there by telling the people about their failings.
He goes into the synagogue, a place of religion, and condemns the
city. Everyone repents of their sins and follows him, right?

Actually, nobody repents of their sins or follows his ideas. Paul's
tirade accomplishes nothing more than earning an invitation from
a few philosophers, who seem to have a hunch that he might be
onto something. They invite him to the Areopagus, a place where
ideas are debated, tempers sometimes flare, and fights occasionally break out—basically the first-century version of my Facebook
wall. On the way, Paul has a change in tactics.

Rather than lambast the Athenians for their sinfulness, Paul
looks past the idols to see what God is doing in the city. "I have
walked to and fro in your city and see that you are a very religious
people." There is a huge difference between calling someone "idol-
atrous sinner" and recognizing that person as "very religious."
He uses their culture as a springboard for conversation. Perhaps
God is not completely absent from Athens after all. "I saw an idol
marked 'to an unknown God.'" Then he leans in. "Let me tell you
about that God."

Hall: This story in Acts is beautiful for so many reasons. Not only does it show the power of God in Paul's transformation from radicalized, violent ideologue to generous, inclusive apostle, but it points again to the nondualistic evangelical practice you were talking about earlier. In conversations with the Athenian philosophers, Paul must be deeply culturally competent; he must listen deeply; *and* he must say something. To leave out any of those parts is to practice a less than full, immature evangelism. For some conservative folks, who've thought of evangelism as telling people exactly what to believe about God, there must be an increased humility and focus on listening and asking questions. For some mainline/liberal folks, who have worshipped that quote attributed to St. Francis, "Preach the gospel at all times; use words only if necessary," there must be an increased boldness to actually say something about God. In the urban American, Millennial "None" context, words will be increasingly necessary.

No condemnation. No "us" and "them." Just people trying to figure out God together. Toward the end of his sermon, he ups the ante on recognizing the presence of God in all things. He tells them, "This is the God 'in whom we live and move and have our being.'" That line is not from the Hebrew Bible. It's from popular Greek poetry. Paul exhibits more than just cultural relevance. He lifts up what is happening in the world around him, recognizes Christ, and points to it in the course of ministry. He demonstrates exactly what it means to assume the omnipresence of God.

If we assume that God is already doing something in the lives of those around us, then everyone is to some degree a pastor. Everyone is a collaborator with Christ. These experiences have led us to one crucial maxim for our ministry: Look for God in others, and they will see God in you.

Susan arrived at Union, looking for a place to sit and paint watercolor. She was a starving artist. Homeless in Dallas, she slept nights on couches of friends—including members of Union's community. The young artist first sat down in our coffee shop with a paintbrush, watercolors, and a stack of paper that would soon become works of art. Sometimes she paints her way through worship gatherings, sometimes through the afternoon coffee shop din of gossip, music, and meetings. Susan doesn't see God in many places in the world, or maybe she sees God in all places. If you pinned her down and forced her to claim a religion, she very well might pick paganism just to throw off the inquirer. Still, Susan is a part of our community. She helped paint a banner we sent to Emanuel AME Church in Charleston following the death of nine members by a gunman. She plans to perform in our Sunday night worship gathering. Susan does not buy in to Christianity, but it's clear to us at Union that God has bought in to her so we treat her as someone who has something to teach us about the God we love.

Out of the blue, she sent me a Facebook message:

> Today I move into my own apartment. There are many people to thank for this monumental regaining of my own space and independence, but you and everyone at Union has a hand in my success. I might seem tough, crazy, and raw, but in my heart of hearts I am a lost soul that desperately needed someone to tell me it's ok to rest here, that I am accepted for all that I am, and need change for no one. I can do anything, and have before, but this last go nearly took it out of me. So from all that I am, thank you all for the spiritual home I was looking for.

We keep looking for God in people like Susan, and they consistently see God in us. Now, she works as a barista on the frontlines of our ministry. The benefit from this kind of work is not just in organic, conversational ways like what we've experienced with Susan. We employ ministries and programs to accomplish this goal.

Getting Naked

On Friday nights, Union hosts a storytelling and spoken-word poetry stage. We celebrate brave vulnerability by asking people to perform "naked"—no props, no notes, nothing on the screen. By offering a setting for stories from the community, we help break down the silos that divide students from the workforce, young professionals from seasoned veterans, nursing students from med school students, as well as any number of other racial, professional, and demographic distinctions that insulate subcommunities in Dallas from one another.

We celebrate stories from our neighborhood. The stage is uncensored, which gives us the credibility to share stories of faith and discipleship. If we told these stories on a Sunday morning, people would swear that they are sermons. Because we tell these stories of faith on an uncensored stage alongside any other story, we have the opportunity to preach to people who don't go to church—simply by celebrating their story.

> **Harrison:** And when you celebrate my story, you celebrate me!

After years of credibility building with members of the local arts community who frequently attend and tell stories on our stage, we are finally seeing some of them check out our worship gatherings and join our congregations. Building credibility with those who have been burned by the church is a long game. Even if nobody who attended the Naked Stage ever connected with our worshipping congregations, however, I'd still consider it a success. We established the Naked Stage to connect neighbors, offer an alternative to the typical Friday night, and find more places where God is at work in the world.

Celebrating Culture in Worship

I generally assume that how a community worships will frame how it lives out its ministry. Therefore, we find ways to celebrate the omnipresence of God in our two weekly worship gatherings. Though each service has its own character, both utilize music that is not overtly religious. The radio is our hymnal and Tuesday night worship gathering features hymns written by Coldplay, Katy Perry, X Ambassadors, Dawes, Imagine Dragons, Bastille, and more. We sing these songs together and celebrate God's message in what others might call secular artists. On Sunday nights, we try to connect with the Dallas Arts Community as well as young professional consultants. We invite local artists to perform and innovators to share their story in the midst of worship. These performances and stories are not overtly religious but somehow connect with the message of the day. When we celebrate communion, I make sure to incorporate words spoken by the performers and innovators into the liturgy. We lift up their work as holy.

We do, of course, critique culture. In a room full of millennials, nothing gets a free pass. What we have found, however, is that in the face of a generation that prides itself on snark, looking for God in all things has led to a progressive change in many of our worship participants. As the church demonstrates its ability to be less cynical of the world around us, young church refugees become less cynical about the church. When we, as a church, own our shortcomings and accept the fact that we might need to learn from the world around us, our customers and congregation become more willing to own their shortcomings and look to the church for help.

> **Harrison:** It lends an authenticity to who we are as the church.

Toward a New Practice of Church

We did not establish Union to bring God to the neighborhood or Christ into the lives of the people who walked through our doors, but nonetheless many of the sixty thousand–plus people who walked through our doors last year are more aware of the presence of God than they were before, because we have looked for God in them and they have seen God in us. The church has learned from what God is actively doing outside its walls, and the Dallas community is beginning to see Union as a vehicle for positive change, regardless of our affiliation as a church.

This practice of looking for God in others expands beyond individual interactions into our corporate relationships with surrounding communities. Despite the fact that Christianity encourages the virtue of humility, the church rarely demonstrates it to the world. When we as church see a need, we tend to tackle it alone. We do not engage in local government, nonprofits, or the business world to make a bigger difference. We exclude others from the opportunity to be a part of God's work, because they might not call it God's work. We worry about who will get the credit and whether or not the other organizations are corrupt, forgetting that God will not be defined by our ecclesiastical boundaries. It's time to be team players. It's time to work alongside other organizations to make our neighborhoods better.

> **Harrison:** Yes! I need to work on this. We cannot live in isolation. This is establishing lifelines for the church and the people.

Toward a New Practice of Pastor

While laboring continuously to acknowledge the presence of God
has changed the way I pastor, it has also changed me as a pastor.
Labor is the right word, because it is not always easy to see God at
work in some people. Adopting this perspective isn't easy, but it is
good. I've become less critical of others, more patient. I've become
kinder to strangers and those who are difficult to work with. I've
become more empowering of people in my care, and consequently,
Union accomplishes far more than it ever could when driven by me
alone. Most important, I've become much more awe-full.

Every day, I get to search.

Every day, I get to listen to stories.

Every day, I get to celebrate what God is doing in others.

Every day, I get to see the face of God in the most unexpected
places.

I can't imagine ministry getting much better than that.

One Pastor and One Location Are Enough to Launch a Church

TREY HALL, URBAN VILLAGE CHURCH

An Alternative Vision

One of the very few burning bush experiences I've had in my life was waking up in the middle of the night on a fall 2007 retreat for leaders interested in the changing shape of twenty-first-century Christianity and feeling God ask me to start a church. God's post-midnight voice was not as clear or commanding—or as verbal, if I'm honest—as what Moses heard on the slopes of Mt. Sinai, but it was significant enough that I couldn't go back to sleep. For a little while I stared at the ceiling, which became a canvas for my imagination. Eventually I sat up, turned on the bedside lamp, and in a euphoric surge of divine hypergraphia, filled a pad of paper with ideas, questions, and the first impressionistic visions of what a new church could look like.

My good friend Christian Coon, another pastor who was on the retreat, confided in me that he had also been feeling some divine nudges around church planting. While we were talking about our

Trey Hall is the cofounding pastor for Urban Village Church in Chicago, Illinois. ◆ urbanvillagechurch.org

individual ideas, Christian asked, out of the blue, "Do you think God might be asking us to do something together?"

Full disclosure: my initial *internal* response was something like, "Uh, thanks for the offer, but I've already got a project that God has given to me." This was less than twenty-four hours after my burning bush experience, so of course I'd already had plenty of time to turn a numinous invitation from God into a sewn-up, me-centered plan.

Thankfully, God has always been readily available to work on my inflated ego, and in the moment following Christian's question, God strengthened the filter between my head and my mouth so that instead of gushing out my internal response of "It's all about me," I said, "Wow. That sounds like something we should explore."

> **Garber:** And I thought I was the only one whose over-inflated ego is used by God!

This was the first of many times in church planting when I've been invited to slow down and take stock before running toward a shiny new thing.

Over the next several months, Christian and I did explore together. We wondered, we prayed, we studied scripture, we took field trips and attended conferences, we talked with our spouses and spiritual directors—all of which helped us to feel out the contours of a project that we became convinced God was asking us to launch. We wrote down the vision, and then, on Pentecost 2008, we submitted to our Conference leadership a proposal for a new church movement in Chicago that would be fueled by three passionate commitments.

First, we wanted to create a new community that would be evangelical (in the deepest sense of the word) and radically inclusive at the same time.

> **Miofsky:** Yes! At The Gathering we wanted to be unapologetically evangelical while at the same time including those often excluded by the church.

We were frustrated with the rigid exclusivity of many of the evangelicals around theology, gender, and sexuality and the suffocatingly refined Jesus-squeamishness of many of the mainliners, and so we wanted to start a gospel-inclusive church that would be powered by the best of both traditions (an idea that is nothing new, but actually quite first-century).

Second, we wanted to create a new community that would *continue* to create new communities. We wanted to become a multisite church that would use rented or borrowed space to launch new sites of our church in different neighborhoods in Chicago and that would eventually resource other churches that are planting congregations in Chicago, across the United States, and even throughout the world.

Third, we wanted to create this new community *together*. Like Paul and Barnabas. Like Mary and Elizabeth. Like the teams of two that Jesus sent out in Luke 10 to announce the kingdom of God in every town and place. We wanted to start a new church together not only because we really liked each other and thought it'd be fun but also because, in all that ethnographic research and field-tripping and scripture studying we did before we wrote down the vision, we came to realize that team ministry is a pattern that you see in almost every healthy, fruitful, interesting church.

> **Miofsky:** Not everyone will have the resources to have two pastors out of the gates, but all of us should prepare for the loneliness and guard against trying to do this all by ourselves.

We wanted to create a community that would view teams as the norm, not only in the pastoral and staff leadership but also in every arena of the life of the church.

You have heard it said . . .

Soon after submitting our proposal, we received a very thoughtful response from the leadership of our Conference. I must say that, quite unlike many of the horror stories I've heard from church planters in other places and traditions who are trying to navigate the internecine bureaucracies and triangulated personalities of some denominational judicatories, our Conference leadership was (and has continued to be) extremely open, committed, and collegial from the beginning.

> **Miofsky:** If you give your Conference leadership a chance, you may be surprised at how willing they are to support new ideas. It is a huge mistake to write judicatory support off before giving it a chance to be helpful.

In their initial response to our proposal, they were generally affirming of the gospel-inclusive part of the vision, but they had lots of questions about the multisite and team-ministry dimensions of the vision. Most of their pushback was expressed in variations on the common theme and conventional wisdom, "One Pastor and One Location Are Enough to Launch a Church":

- "Why would we need two pastors to start this community?"
- "At the beginning of the project, you would have so few people to pastor. There would hardly be enough work for one pastor, actually hardly enough work for a halftime or quarter-time pastor. What would the two of you do all day?"

- "Which one of you would be in charge? Who would be the lead pastor and who would be the associate pastor? Who would actually call the shots?"
- "Wouldn't it be smarter to send one of you to start a church in one part of the city and the other of you to start a different church in another part of the city?"
- "How would two sites in totally different neighborhoods be connected as one church?"

Miofsky: Church planters should expect these kinds of logistical questions from funders and potential supporters. These "how" questions can squelch your passion, but they can also help sharpen your vision.

The questions our Conference leadership asked were fair questions, but nevertheless questions that revealed the conventional wisdom, at least according to mainline Christianity, both for what a church is supposed to look like and for what a pastor is supposed to do. This has become conventional wisdom, of course, because it has been conventional practice for a long time. In most American contexts, "One Pastor and One Location Are Enough" is standard operating procedure.

And it's standard operating procedure because, in the contexts of many existing congregations, it has made decent sense. The great majority of American churches are small—fewer than one hundred people—and have been small for a long time. The small size means that one pastor makes for a very manageable pastor-parishioner ratio (especially given the chaplaincy model of pastoral authority that is frequently part of smaller church culture), a feasible financial reality (often the pastor is the only employee), and a lean clarity about who's responsible for interpreting the church's mission and ministry ("Got a question? Ask the pastor").

Having one location—focusing mission and ministry in only one town, area, or neighborhood—makes sense, too. Every context is complex, and it takes time to understand the multivalence of an area—its histories, current realities, shifting demographics and developments, and most importantly, the power that connects or disconnects them all. Developing a neighborhood exegesis and power analysis also takes energy. Focusing ministry in one place can help the congregation and pastor to steward missional time and energy well, be savvy about concentrating efforts of evangelism and outreach for maximum effect, and prevent the dissipation of energy that occurs when a congregational system is spread too thin. (We must also recognize the fact that in many denominations the majority of congregations are tied to old, crumbling buildings that were built a century or more ago for a different experience and practice of church. This presents a long-term challenge that will only exacerbate in the next generation. Congregations where building maintenance or repair is a large and necessary part of the ministry will feel the missional energy deplete dramatically, even as they are focused on only one location.)

Given the historical precedent for the "One Pastor and One Location" model, it's not surprising that even when many denominations kick off a new project—to start a church or to redevelop an existing church—they assume that, instead of embracing a new model for the new project, all they need to do is to supercharge the conventional approach. Quite often this strategy means finding a bright, hardworking, usually young "superstar" solo pastor who is willing to give a hundred hours a week to the project and then parachuting her or him into the territory with a mission to essentially create a pep rally that will turn into something.

Miofsky: Denominational leaders, please do not put young, talented pastors into difficult ministry situations expecting him or her to "turn it around." If you do this, be prepared to support holistic change and give financial and other support. Otherwise, you are really just throwing a Hail Mary, and that is a good way to burn a pastor out.

The success of these supercharged setups is, in most contexts, pretty rare, which is why the successful ones are so church-media worthy. But the statistically low percentage of success with this model (only one in five make it) unfortunately hasn't given us enough pause to change our "conventional wisdom" pedagogy for redevelopment or planting. When Christian and I went to church planting boot camp only seven years ago in 2008, this was still the predominant model offered. When we suggested an alternative model, the pushback from our Conference leadership revealed how deeply ingrained the conventional wisdom is.

But we say to you . . .

We believe that an alternative "More Than One Pastor and More Than One Place" model is a necessary component in any long-term meta strategy for reaching the next generations with the gospel of Jesus Christ. We must explore *teams of leaders* working in *more than one* neighborhood zone as *part of the same church.* This approach is, of course, not a perfect model or the only model for twenty-first-century church starting and redevelopment, but it should at least be a partner model in most contexts, and in a few contexts it might actually be the best model.

Miofsky: We embody multisite differently at The Gathering but have arrived at the same conclusions.

I'm happy to report that after several months of generous back-and-forth with our Conference leadership, many more sleepless nights, lots more questions and apparently enough cogent answers to be convincing, Christian and I were sent to plant together. In July 2009, almost two years after God asked us to start a new church, we left our previous congregations to begin a mutual project that would eventually become Urban Village Church. Currently our church operates in four worship sites, with more than twenty-five small groups, in diverse neighborhoods in the city of Chicago. We are approximately eight hundred adults and children strong, with 90 percent of our membership from the Millennial Generation or Generation X. What started as a two-pastor team is now a four-pastor team that also includes a full-time director of discipleship and director of operations who serve the entire Urban Village movement. While we've been growing in our neighborhoods, seven of the student pastors or clergy residents who have come alongside of us during our first six years to learn about church starting have gone on to launch new communities in other places.

As we survey the first six years of planting with this alternative model, we humbly offer some of the gifts—and their accompanying challenges—that God has given us.

Gift of "More Than One Pastor" #1: Diversity of Leadership

Having more than one pastor or representative leader builds an essential diversity into the congregational culture from the beginning. Christian and I have a shared vision for the church, but we cast and lead that vision from very different places. One of us is an extrovert; one of us is an introvert. One of us preaches more celebratively; one of us preaches more contemplatively. One of us is straight; one of us is gay. One of us is more creative; one of us is more strategic. As Urban Village has grown, we have tried to increase our leadership diversity with regard to gender, race, and ethnicity; theological perspective; sexual orientation; gender identity, and so forth.

Baughman: Lacking multiple staff members at my church, I've relied heavily on a diverse leadership team of volunteers. I generally find that, in church work, your congregation will reflect your leadership. I've seen a lot of churches start a new worship service for young people that is led by a team of baby boomers who like to wear jeans. Guess who shows up? Boomers who like to wear jeans. The leadership in my church is made up entirely of our target demographic—including people who don't believe in God, because that is part of the community to whom we desperately want to connect.

The congregation has benefited from this: people who would have never felt connected to the church through my ministry are part of the church because they connect with Christian's, or Emily's, or Brittany's, or that of one of the other lay or staff leaders who are part of the many teams. And that's a very, very good thing. Having more than one pastor not only prevents the personality cult that is possible with only one leader but also disrupts the monolithic "homogeneous unit principle" strategy that is the norm in many traditions and tends to create "echo chamber" congregations. Having more than one pastor increases the potential of creating "unity in diversity" congregations with a larger capacity to hold different ideas and to meaningfully integrate them in the mission.

I don't mean to suggest that this is romantic or easy. Urban Village was started by two white men and so it's no surprise that the overall congregation is predominantly white (around 75 percent). As our congregation deepens its commitment to be an increasingly multiethnic, antiracist church and envisions a future when there is no racial majority at Urban Village, we must strengthen our pastoral and lay leadership diversity now in order to lead toward that envisioned future.

> **Miofsky:** This is one of my biggest regrets at The Gathering, that we were not more intentional about racial diversity from the very beginning. It is easier to start with this commitment than to try and change it later.

Gift of "More Than One Pastor" #2: Honesty about Gifts and Limits

Leaders in this kind of team ministry also discover a freedom to offer their gifts and to acknowledge their limits—both of which are important for a healthy system. In a "One Pastor Is Enough" model, the solo pastor can feel pressured to try to be all things to all people, which usually manifests as compulsive overwork and subsequent burnout, the tendency to fake gifts that she or he never was given in order to be perceived as a well-rounded pastor, or a bad case of control freakery.

In a team ministry approach, leaders can experience the joy of doing a few things really well instead of the anxiety of having to do everything adequately well (or not adequately well!); a mutual honesty about the limits of their own identities and competencies; and a more flexible congregational and staff strategy that is built on a mature, non-defensive assessment of what is actually possible with the players at the table.

> **Miofsky:** Amen. The sooner I recognized what I was not good at, the sooner I was able to build a staff and lay team to address those areas.

This freedom is beneficial not only for the church as a whole but also for each pastor. Personally, I have experienced deep transformation through team relationship with my trusted colleagues. This transformation, at the outset, can be scary and foreign: to release the control freakery that is implicitly taught as an important ministry practice brings up all kinds of fear and uncertainty buried just below the ego's surface. However, as you learn to let go of your leadership compulsions and welcome the saving truth that you are neither the headquarters of the universe nor the nerve center of the church, the transformation that occurs becomes utterly life-giving, because you are not the only one undergoing the transformation: your team is undergoing it together.

Gift of "More Than One Pastor" #3: Long-Term Stability

The alternative wisdom of "More Than One Pastor" can also diminish the potential of congregational stagnation or mission breakdown when there is a significant transition in pastoral or staff leadership. While I have deep respect for the superstar clergy in my own denomination who have built very large movements as the solo or chief leader, I also wonder what will happen when they retire, resign, or simply move on to the next thing.

Leadership transition is never easy, but it is much less debilitating when a congregation has been shaped not by the vision and charisma of one woman or man but by the vision and charisma of several women and men on a dynamic and flexible pastoral team. When one of the pastors leaves Urban Village, it will be hard and painful, of course, but it will not fundamentally shift the congregation's vision and movement, which have always been about—and have always been led by—more than one person.

Gift of "More Than One Place" #1: Big and Small at the Same Time

A multisite church model, in which a congregation is understood fundamentally to be serving in more than one place, can hold together the powerful critical mass of a movement with the intimacy of a close community. Such a model can be both big and small at the same time—a third way between the false binary of either mega-church or family-sized church. At Urban Village Church, each of our four sites is in the range of only 100–250 participants—small enough for people to know each other well, to get easily connected to a ministry area and small group, and to worship as a member of a participating congregation as opposed to a viewing audience. Our practiced value of intimacy at the site level means that people can potentially experience church as a community of sisters and brothers.

That said, as one church movement, more than eight hundred strong, we are large enough to be a significant force for social change in our city and denomination, to enjoy the relative financial security that can be more elusive in smaller churches, and to exercise a more expansive evangelistic reach. The practiced value of power at the larger movement level means that we can turn out fifty people to the state capitol (two hundred miles from Chicago) to advocate for issues of justice that the gospel calls us to care about, assemble 125 people to march at the LGBTQ Pride Parade and pass out invitations to the party of Jesus, and support bold projects that would be more difficult or even impossible without the "common pot" approach of sharing financial resources between sites.

Gift of "More Than One Place" #2: One Mission, Locally Adapted

A multisite church can also model a way of at once embracing a strong common mission across the movement and expecting the particular incarnation of that mission to look different, depending on the neighborhood context of each site. A strong mission is a flexible mission: indigenous expression and hyper local nuancing of a strong mission do not dilute the power of that mission; on the contrary, they increase its power and embolden its truth.

One of the valid critiques of church starting in general and multisite church staring in particular is that, especially when practiced by majority white, wealthy congregations, the planting activity can be unconsciously or consciously colonialistic. It would be easy to convey one experience or interpretation of the gospel as if it is *the* experience or interpretation of the gospel, and therefore act more like agents of gentrification or white supremacy than agents of the ever-expanding, more-than-one-expression, inclusive gospel of Jesus Christ. A cookie-cutter, one-size-fits-all approach that some multisite churches unreflectively employ can be insensitive and even harmful in diverse contexts. For example, practitioners of video venue preaching have to be especially sensitive to this tendency and to think through ways to disrupt the hegemony of one (usually white, straight male) leader's proclamation of the gospel being piped into every worship service of the multisite church.

Miofksy: We utilize video preaching but supplement it with live-site pastor preaching as well. This allows each site to hear a diversity of voices even while we take advantage of some of the benefits of technology.

But a multisite church doesn't have to be that way. At Urban Village, we expect our mission ("To Create Jesus-Loving, Inclusive Communities That Ignite the City") to evoke diverse responses from each site's leadership, depending on the needs, questions, and hopes of the people they serve in the neighborhoods they live and gather in. What are the embedded artistic, musical expressions of that neighborhood, and how might the praise of God look different in worship if those expressions are taken into account? What about the social traditions: how are human relationships formed and built in that context? What are the particular cries for justice from that neighborhood? What keeps people awake at night? How do institutional power histories and current realities around political leadership and decision-making affect the neighborhood? Given the neighborhood's demographics, who is missing from the church's membership and why are they missing? Only an indigenous site leadership with a deep consciousness of these realities and the authority to interpret the mission of the entire church for that context will be able to critically engage and answer those questions in order to then build a faithful, relevant ministry plan around the responses.

Gift of "More Than One Place" #3: Ongoing Research and Development

A church in more than one place participates in a dynamic system that encourages learning from risk, improvisation, and even failure. The synergy of multisite church planting builds "research and development" into the very heart of the project. In a church in only one place, there's a perception that everything will be on the line with any proposed shift in strategy; such a perception (which may or may not be actually true) increases anxiety and therefore diminishes the potential of experimentation. But a church in more than one place is used to trying new things (there wouldn't be more than one site if they hadn't risked at least once!) and this experience informs future endeavors. When one site tries something new and succeeds, all the other sites of the church benefit from the success, gaining both new information and new spiritual energy that they would not have received if they were disconnected solo sites.

On the other hand, when a site tries something new and fails, all of the other sites offer spiritual and material support in the midst of the failure. For example, I helped launch and was the primary staff leader for Urban Village's second site. We launched on Sunday nights in a beautiful old Lutheran sanctuary. We had more than 130 people at our launch, and we were thrilled. Over the next eighteen months, for reasons I still don't entirely understand, we slowly bled energy and attendance. To make the loss feel less painful and obvious, we moved our worship service from the vast sanctuary to the smaller parlor and then again to the smaller basement. Meanwhile, we were trying everything we knew to turn around the decline. We were preaching up a storm—the same sermons from our growing Sunday morning site in a different neighborhood. We were going door-to-door and inviting people in the neighborhood. We retooled our strategy a couple times, training up new leaders, reconfiguring teams, redesigning worship. And still there was that same damn slow leak, which continued to drain our purpose and passion all the way through our last season, when we were lucky to get twenty-five folks in that grotty church basement.

Our site leaders came together to discern what to do. We knew that we needed to change the game, but how? Should we totally close up shop? Just try harder to find more people or a better preacher or a better band? In midst of the conversation, through prayer and the support of colleagues and leaders from other sites (during the second site's slow leak, Urban Village had planted a third site that was growing fast) we came to understand that our failure, while painful, was nothing to be ashamed of.

> **Garber:** If only more churches could be this bold . . . to launch another site while one is dying.

We had tried our best and offered it to God. Once we experienced the freedom of that knowledge, we decided that we could take another risk and try again. We relaunched three months later on Sunday mornings in a different venue and have been growing steadily ever since, eventually becoming Urban Village's largest and youngest site. But none of that—the gift of not feeling ashamed, the chance to try something radically new, the opportunity to learn from it—would have been possible without the support of the other sites.

> **Miofsky:** This is an important lesson on failing fast and forward. As planters, we will likely have as many failures as successes, so learning to weather them and learn from them is essential.

One Final Word

If I had the opportunity to add a couple of characteristics to the official lists of the marks of the church or the fruits of the Holy Spirit, I'd suggest *boldness, fun,* and *not being boring.* When Jesus tells us to be the salt of the earth, I like to imagine that those are some of the qualities he has in mind.

The alternative wisdom of the "More Than One Pastor and More Than One Place" model won't be directly applicable in every context, of course. But whatever your setting, I challenge you to seriously consider giving some version of it a try. If you gather a team of diverse, gospel-powered people and envision a project that is more weather system than rain shower, it will be fun, it will be bold, and most assuredly it will not be boring. You may succeed.

You may fail. If you're like most of us, probably you'll do both. But wherever you end up, what you learn will change the way you do church, for good, for the rest of your ministry.

Garber: This is Jesus-like genius right here.

Polished Excellence Draws Young People

AMANDA GARBER, RISE

You have heard it said . . .

Even the donuts were perfect. They were arranged in a flawless spiral on the large, colorful, handcrafted pottery tray. Next to the locally sourced donuts, clearly baked by angels, were three fair trade coffee blends with organic creamer and sugar. In the middle of the breakfast spread (which made my hotel's offering hang its head in shame) stood an enormous bouquet of stunning wildflowers arranged flawlessly in a Caribbean-water-colored glass vase. I overheard a young woman casually comment, "Oh those? I was in a huge rush, picked those this morning on my way out the door and threw them together. You should have seen last week's flowers, because they were waaaayyyy better." Waaaaayyyy better, indeed. Everything about this place was waaaayyy better.

> **Herships:** Perfection bores me. I like what Tom Waits says: "What I do is kind of abstract. I break a lot of eggs, and I leave the shell

---

Amanda Garber is the pastor of RISE in Harrisonburg, Virginia. ◆ riseharrisonburg.com

in there. Texture is everything." No one really likes *all* the colors inside the lines because we can't relate, and truly, we don't like those people that much anyway.

The year was 2010, and a new, Jesus-as-renegade vision had taken root within the almost fifty-year-old, remarkably mediocre campus ministry known as the Wesley Foundation at James Madison University. The entire ministry was journeying through a season of "holy agitation," and its leaders could sense that change was coming. I found myself on a roller coaster of creativity that was frequently inebriating and occasionally vomit-inducing. To deal with the dizzying experience, I started searching for new friends and information. Since it seemed like some sort of new community was getting ready to be born out of our campus ministry, logic dictated that I visit other new faith communities that were a little more seasoned and generally smarter than we were. Turns out, they were not hard to find. I needed new friends who knew how to plant churches that "appeal to" young adults. Now, back to the donuts . . .

On Sunday morning I found myself in a lobby of an elementary school, amazed by the breakfast that clearly was catered by Martha Stewart. It was a beautiful thing: the donuts, fresh fruit, coffee, flowers, extra-perky greeters. We were efficiently and subtly moved through the lobby to our seats. Everything was flawless. The lighting, the perfect segues, the band in their hipster glasses and skinny jeans, the stirring message, the folks who casually approached me, asked my name, and then somehow within the span of two minutes enabled me to feel instantly connected to this community, its mission, and its donuts. *How did they do it?*

It was magic, I tell you. Disney-type magic flowed throughout this place. I scanned the room and saw hundreds of young faces, hands raised and bodies swaying during the worship songs, tears streaming down their cheeks, and eager faces hanging on the pastor's every syllable. They even searched for dollars, cents, and PayPal during the not-too-manipulative-but-still-really-convincing plea for financial support. Hell, even I, the spying pastor, gave more than I expected to. Those were some powerful donuts.

One could only surmise that the lives in this church plant were being changed. I wasn't completely sure what my embryonic community would look like, but I was pretty sure I wanted it to look and feel like this. In fact, I wanted this moment, this experience, to last forever. In case you are wondering, it didn't.

But I say to you . . .

The perfect donut-inspired moment did not last because those moments never do. And, it didn't, mostly because my beloved "embryonic community," named RISE, developed at warp speed and took its first breath in 2010. Suddenly, stuff got real. I quickly realized that much like newborn humans, newborn communities are simultaneously breathtaking, exhausting, and transformational. One can't help but fall madly in love with them, quirks and all. They are extremely needy, keep you up at night, and even smell like spit-up and poop sometimes, but illogically, you love them. And, much like the humans I have birthed, my beloved community has invited me to slowly and sometimes begrudgingly release my need for certainty, neatness, and flawless flowers.

I do not mean to criticize or begrudge anyone who serves a well-choreographed, well-lit, delectable-donuts kind of church. I can only admire the amount of effort, rehearsal time, and dedication required by that community. Still, in the interest of full disclosure, I must admit that a part of me will always long for the "perfect" Sunday morning. I am not usually one for spiritual warfare-type language, but if I had a "demon-in-chief," her name would be Perfectionism. She would consume only fair-trade coffee and wear skinny jeans. Her highlights would be impeccable, and her messages would make people laugh, cry, and want to become a part of it. She wouldn't "try too hard," because she would just naturally be *that* cool. Sing it with me, now. *"I wish that I could be like the cool kids . . ."*

At this point, I hope you are laughing, or at least grinning. (Remember, I want to make you laugh, cry, and become a part of it.) I also hope you are sensing my irony, and maybe, just maybe, you are relating a bit.

> **Herships:** I *am* relating! Even after five years, every Monday night I still feel like the kid in eighth grade, throwing the birthday party and wondering if anybody's going to show up. Then I end up hating myself because I actually care if they do.

I wake up most days wondering how we can change the world by God's grace. Some days, I am sincere, authentic, and passionate. Some days, I struggle with a deep need for validation and affirmation. Like most of us, I am well aware of one of the "rules" of church planting: If you want people to show up, especially people under age thirty, then you'd better put on a good show. If you build it, and it is perfect, they will come. Many of the experts, supervisor types, and gurus in my neck of the woods speak frequently of "excellence." Be excellent. Get the young people. It's that simple.

> **Jacobs:** *If reaching young people is that simple then our problem is solved, right?* I wish it was that simple.

I could offer many theories about why nice American, appropriate, high-achieving upper-middle-class church folks created and embrace the myth that "shiny is superior." I could ask lots of provocative questions like, What does "excellence" look like in the kingdom of God? Who or what are we *really* worshipping here? Do fog machines really transform lives? WCWJD? (What coffee would Jesus drink?) I simply will say, however, that when my lifelong struggle with the "never-quite-good-enough" voices intersected with a church culture that often worships excellence, well . . . let's just say I am now the owner of three pairs of skinny jeans.

Herships: I am the proud owner of at *least* four pairs of APC jeans. I know people say they don't care what other people think. You know what? That may be the cool way to respond, but I don't think we ever completely stop wanting to be fully accepted . . . and put on ridiculous masks to help us achieve it. Then I think of a sentiment growing popularity: "Be yourself . . . everyone else is taken."

When I was pregnant with both of my children, I felt remarkably ill-equipped to cross the threshold of parenthood. In order to parent well, I needed research. (Oh, who am I kidding? I didn't simply want to parent "well," I wanted to parent with *excellence*.) I spent those gestational seasons closely studying babies, children, and their parents. Thus, when I discovered something that seemed effective or helpful, I took note. Baby carriers that enable the parental figure to have his or her hands free at all times? Check. A gadget that keeps baby wipes warm so that the infant's tushie doesn't have to withstand the shock of a room-temperature diaper change? Check. I was ready. Or, so I thought.

I often compare the journey of church planting to pregnancy and parenthood. Thus, I approached planting RISE in a fashion similar to my other gestational research. I studied other relatively new faith communities, their planters, their best practices, and so on. (Remember the story about me and the donuts?) When one is creating something from nothing, hand-in-hand with God, it's helpful to have a few images, phrases, and ideas in the back pocket of one's skinny jeans. So, when RISE's launch team started dreaming about what our first worship service, our "launch," might look and feel like, I drew from visits to numerous faith communities and some Internet experts, too.

> **Jacobs:** This reminds me of what we did at my church. In our case we also visited numerous faith communities in order to help us create something different yet still engaging and empowering instead of offering what every other church was offering.

I used my "woo" and I convinced my launch team, which at that time consisted of twelve people all under the age of twenty-five, that we needed to be excellent, shiny, and well-produced. Several of my launch team folks pushed back a bit and questioned that plan. We engaged in a number of meaningful conversations about identity, authenticity, and a Jesus-type understanding of "excellence." We wrestled with what it means to "attract" young adults. Is there a difference between attracting people and forming disciples? Ultimately, the powerful and seductive desire to be one of the "cool kids" proved victorious. We wanted young adults to come, so we followed "the rule." We would be cool.

And, God laughed. Really hard.

RISE worship launched in the basement of The Blue Nile, an Ethiopian restaurant in Downtown Harrisonburg, Virginia. The basement of the Nile was a bar. It was cool in a grungy, interesting, hipster sort of way. It was well-known and a bit "notorious" in young adult circles around town. The Nile was exactly where we needed to begin our journey as a faith community, primarily because it branded us in important ways. It forced us to become nimble, craft an excellent sense of humor, and master helpful skills like toilet plunging as well as cleaning up broken glass, urine, and cigarette butts.

> **Jacobs:** Church planters have to do it all, from preaching to praying to picking up trash and cleaning the toilets. Gotta love it!

The Nile mocked our attempts to pose as the cool kids. It invited us to a more authentic, vulnerable posture.

I will never forget week three. We had two fairly solid worship experiences under our belt, so obviously, we were almost experts. The previous two weeks had offered a few "hiccups" but nothing we couldn't handle with energy, teamwork, and well-crafted lattes. Week three was less of a "hiccup" and more of a long, painful belch.

A few seconds after walking through the doors that morning, I could sense that the worship seas might be a bit choppy. Turns out, a worship typhoon was heading our way. The power worked intermittently throughout the morning. When the power was on, nothing, and I mean nothing, functioned technologically. Toilets overflowed. Numerous strands of Christmas lights that the nightclub had loosely duct taped to the ceiling in September started falling on people during the message, resulting in a fair amount of surprise and flailing from worshipers. I knew that the entire morning was almost lost, but I was determined to save it with the best, most stirring consecration of the Communion elements anyone, anywhere had ever experienced. I gave it my all. As I started speaking, though, I heard something playing faintly in the background. It was music that bore a striking resemblance to the theme from the iconic movie *2001: A Space Odyssey.* I decided to simply talk louder, because I would not be defeated by extraterrestrials or whoever had decided to kill our worship vibe. The more I projected and pretended that the mother ship wasn't landing, the louder the music became. Our leaders, confused and desperate to salvage something from the morning, jumped up and attempted to subtly move around the room in an effort to search and destroy the source of this bizarre music. Normally, ten people meandering around the room might have proven distracting. Thankfully, most of those present were infinitely more distracted by the fact that Christmas lights continued to fall on their heads while extremely dramatic music (buuuuummmm buuuuummmm buuuuummmm . . . BUM BUM!) reverberated throughout the basement. Did I mention the toilets kept overflowing?

Turns out, the employee who was setting up for Sunday brunch upstairs in the restaurant area of the Nile was unaware that 120-ish folks were downstairs. So, she decided to turn on some loud, stirring, spaceship-landing type music while she completed her pre-brunch checklist. She also was unaware that any music turned on upstairs also was heard downstairs. Mystery solved.

Jacobs: This reminds me of what happened at my church. We are located in a storefront. I remember it was a hot July summer day. I arrived at the church at 7 a.m. only to discover that the power was out as a result of copper thieves. I thought all hope was lost. Panic filled my mind. What will people say? How will we have worship? Will people worship in the dark without air-conditioning, etc.? Then the most powerful thing happened as persons on the leadership team came together, and before you know it a plan was in place and then executed. Cold water showed up as well as generators to help power the instruments, fans, and more. We ended up having one of our most powerful worship experiences at The Village since launch. Even when it looks like all hope is lost, God still makes a way.

My memory becomes somewhat blurry after the crescendo of Communion. I remember apologizing a lot and asking people to "give us another chance next week." I am pretty sure we forgot to collect an offering. We stumbled through a final song and our worship leader's parting words were, "Let's get out of here." I could not have agreed more.

Jared stood in the way of my escape. Every community needs a prophet (or two, or ten). Ours was an Eastern Mennonite Seminary student named Jared. He was a bit of a peculiar character, because he wasn't plagued by my/our "we must find a way to be cool" complex. He asked brilliant questions . . . the type Jesus would ask. As I sat on the edge of the stage that fateful morning, with my head in my hands, convinced no one would ever return for worship and that all hope was lost, he sat down next to me and said, "Please stop apologizing. No one begrudges you for being human. This morning offered others permission to be less than perfect, more human, more authentic. This morning, RISE started to feel like real community for me, and I am gonna guess that is true for others, too."

The prophet Jared was right. People did return the next Sunday, and the Sunday after that, and they still show up every Sunday at exactly 10-ish.

> **Baughman:** This rings true from my experiences at Union as well. We have had *scripted* introductions that still go off the rails, Prayers of Confession that forget to ask for forgiveness, more technology errors than I can count, twelve-minute-long "two minute stories," and volunteer worship leaders who have shown up a little inebriated. People seem to come back, though, because of our flaws—as long as we own them and don't pretend they aren't there.

I sometimes marvel at the fact that they continue to show up. To this day, we tell the story of "week three." It's become a part of the RISE narrative, a part of our identity, and a memory that reminds us that though we may try to achieve "well produced" status, we will always and forever be the church where Christmas lights fall on people and spaceships land during the Eucharist.

We've experienced many "week three" moments throughout the past five years. On Easter Sunday 2012, a band member's phone alarm started beeping during the final portion of the Easter sermon. Once again, leaders were searching the theater for the source of this mysterious and remarkably loud sound. This alarm sounded throughout much of the service, and once again, the service went off the rails (only this time, chaos ensued on the most holy day of the year). Fog machine experiences have gone awry, a band member has fallen face-first off of the theater stage, "multi-sensory worship" moments have become way too touchy-feely and awkward, and our band has been . . . *ahem* . . . less than stellar on occasion. Recently, our local firefighters made an appearance halfway through the message. They were dressed in full firefighter gear, complete with axes and walkie-talkies. They didn't explain why they were there and tried to "play it cool." With no explanation, firefighters began crawling around on the floor. Turns out the theater marquee had some sort of a short in it and sparks were flying. Never a dull moment.

I have focused primarily on our worship experiences, but let me assure you that our missional efforts are every bit as unpolished as our Sunday morning gatherings. Fresh produce has decayed and almost fermented in backpacks that we've attempted to deliver to hungry children in our community. One of our college students once drove a van full of at-risk elementary school children into the corner of the RISE Mission House (obviously Jesus should have taken the wheel). We've had four hundred people show up for events when we expected one hundred, and we've had twenty-five show up when we expected 150. When that happens, we usually panic. It's all good.

> **Jacobs:** I know how you feel. We spent hours planning what we thought would draw hundreds of people only to have a handful show up. One event we had two hundred subway sandwiches donated for an outreach event. We had ten people show up. Needless to say, the team was eating subway sandwiches for a week.

We are remarkably human, and maybe that's the essence, the beauty, the "draw" of RISE. My messages sometimes resonate deeply, and sometimes they are remarkably underwhelming. Our donuts are not always delectable; in fact, sometimes they are the small, powdered ones that come cheaper by the dozen and are first cousins with the Twinkie. Our greeters are not always enthusiastic or "on fire" (unless they accidentally back into the candles). In fact, we count it a "win" if they arrive on time and have brushed their hair and teeth. We frequently hold things together with duct tape. Our leaders sometimes (okay, often) don't invite friends and neighbors to RISE events. We constantly forget to put the gluten-free Communion option on the table and fill the chalices with grape juice. Almost all of our Communion sets are chipped or cracked (even the wooden ones). One of our guitar players regularly channels his inner Slash and offers startling guitar riffs at unexpected moments in worship. Two children in the community carved their names into the theater bathroom stalls when they should have been creating theologically meaningful crafts out of Popsicle sticks.

What I've shared here may not come as much of a surprise to you. You may follow the millennial expert-gurus who repeatedly state that young adults long for something real, authentic, and vital. We're regularly told they want mystery, authenticity, and meaning, and they have little tolerance for hypocrisy.

Herships: The phoniness of church has left so many people cold and they don't know there is an alternative. And it's not God they have the beef with. I think of the Lenny Bruce quote, "Everyday people are straying from the church and going back to God."

I'm no expert, and I regularly caution against assuming all persons under the age of thirty are carbon copies. However, my personal experience would most certainly underscore the experts' opinions and observations in this regard. While I'm sure there are plenty of young adults seeking "cool" churches and faith communities, I haven't personally encountered many of them. Most of the young adults with whom I've journeyed have little tolerance for shiny, happy church folks and are repelled by the "fake" (their words) nature of many churches. Time and time again, I've heard: "Life is hard enough, so why waste time with people who aren't 'real'? What is most important, after all? What happens when the Jesus bling becomes less shiny over time? What happens 'when the music fades and all is stripped away'?"

I am not advocating for laziness or mediocrity. God knows I have witnessed enough mediocrity and complacency in the church to last beyond a lifetime. However, my beloved community has helped me reimagine "mediocre." Our unexpected journey of grace has enabled me to understand and imagine community in new ways. They've given me a different lens through which I view "perfect" and new ways to measure passion and success. Our "benchmarks" and standards for excellence tend to resemble those of Jesus instead of Western capitalistic culture.

RISE is messy, quirky, and at times, comical. Somehow, though, God's grace powerfully moves through and beyond this community of misfit toys. Countless lives are being transformed. One could argue that God always has had a funny way of calling flawed, goofy, imperfect folks to be about the work of mending creation. I won't claim to understand God, or who or why or when God calls, or how grace moves in such mysterious ways, but I can tell you this: the past five years have enabled me to become a more honest, vulnerable, and truly joyful leader. The laughter, tears, moments of forgiveness, insight gained, backpacks packed, kids mentored, meals packaged, soap and shampoo distributed, assumptions reimagined, and lives transformed have offered a breathtaking glimpse of Jesus's upside down Kingdom.

I will forever cherish the memory of RISE's first Easter celebration during which I shared the true and harrowing tale of "Oops," the monkey who once escaped from the small and quirky zoo in my hometown of Roanoke, Virginia. Oops's escape brought an almost unprecedented sense of excitement to the Star City of the South. Weeks passed and no one could corral Oops; he made appearances all over town, including outside local hospital windows and along the Blue Ridge Parkway. Local news personalities offered daily updates on Oops's supposed whereabouts; he became a bit of a local celebrity. I explored the ways that, much like a renegade monkey, the stubborn, scrappy nature of Resurrection hope has a way of surprising us when we least expect it. The Risen Christ seems to pop up all over the place and is "on the loose." Thus, the refrain throughout that morning was "Hope is on the loose."

My journey with RISE has shown me that the radical Resurrection hope of Jesus cannot be controlled or neatly packaged. It relentlessly comes to us in unexpected ways and through the most unexpected people. Try though we might to manage it and even cage it, it will not be contained. So, friends, are you desiring a polished community with perfect donuts and a worship band so skilled they could produce their own WOW worship CD? Have you bought into the myth that young adults seek only an airbrushed, sparkly community? If so, I get it. I certainly understand if you want to chase "perfect" for a season. Been there, done that. While you are chasing church plant nirvana, though, I invite you to pause at some point and listen closely.

Do you hear that?

That's God laughing at you and with you.

That's God delighting in your passion and desire, albeit at times a wee bit misguided.

That's God chuckling at your stale powdered donuts and half-asleep greeters with bed head.

That's God singing slightly off-key and probably a bit too loud with your band (who just found a last-minute drummer at 11:00 p.m. on Saturday night).

That's God speaking through the unexpected prophets in your midst.

That may even be God attempting to land a spaceship during the Eucharist.

And, that's definitely God whispering, "Hope is on the loose."

Cities Present More Challenges than Opportunities for Church Planting

MATT MIOFSKY, THE GATHERING

You have heard it said . . .

"Matt, we already have fifty-four churches in St. Louis. Why do we need a fifty-fifth?"

> **Brown:** Church planters, get ready for this question, because it is tailor-made for you and your vision to reach new people for Jesus Christ.

Good question. The answer became the vision for The Gathering, the church that I planted in the fall of 2006. Another pastor asked me this question about a year earlier, as I was sharing the idea for a new church in the city of St. Louis.

At that time, United Methodism was just beginning to lift up the value of starting new churches. Most new congregations were planted in fast-growing suburbs that were relatively new and

---

Matt Miofsky is the founding pastor for The Gathering in St. Louis, Missouri. ◆ gatheringnow.org

without a lot of churches. Most of these churches occupied non-traditional space that matched the effort to reach people disconnected from traditional church. All of it made perfect sense. New churches need people, so plant in a growing area. New churches work better where little is happening, so focus on new communities that are not already full of existing churches.

> **Baughman:** This was certainly the prevailing wisdom when I was trained as a church planter. I agree that it is important, but I would hesitate to call it church growth. Most of it is picking up members from churches people left when they moved to a new town. If we really want to grow the church, we need to be in neighborhoods where very few people are going to church and minister with them in ways that other congregations are not.

New churches have to overcome negative perceptions about church, so perhaps nontraditional spaces are best. Traditional mainline churches are largely in decline, so try something different, perhaps more contemporary. All of this made perfect sense.

And yet I found myself discerning a call to start a new church that seemed to cut against all of this popular wisdom. I wanted to plant a church in the city of St. Louis, in a declining neighborhood (at least in population) in an old, traditional church building. While I love St. Louis, nothing about it screams "plant a church," especially not by traditional measures. Since 1950, St. Louis has lost 63 percent of its population. In the last decade alone, the city has lost nearly thirty thousand people. St. Louis just celebrated its 250th anniversary and has little new housing development compared to many growing metropolitan areas.

> **Brown:** It is so important for planters to know the statistics for the neighborhood in which they are planting.

Given that the population is in decline, it stands to reason that new people are not moving here in large numbers. Furthermore, St. Louis is full of churches, many of which are in decline. In business terminology, it is a mature, saturated market. For all those reasons, St. Louis wasn't going to pop up on anyone's top ten list of prime places to plant. It was also probably for this reason that of all the existing United Methodist churches in the city of St. Louis, not one of them was started in the twentieth or twenty-first century. This was a city that planted churches in the late 1800s, during the city's growth period, and essentially stopped planting new churches one hundred years ago.

> **Cunningham:** Can we really expect to reach people in the twenty-first century with models that are over one hundred years old?

Armed with all of that information, I approached my conference leadership in 2006 with a vision to start a new church in the city of St. Louis. The desire to plant a church in the city of St. Louis was downright counterintuitive. The very first issue I had to address was why? Gun-shy from failures, in need of easy wins, and with limited resources, many church leaders appreciated my passion but weren't impressed with the vision. They saw better places to take risks and deploy resources. The objections made perfect sense, and that is precisely why we hadn't yet tried it. It was also precisely why we were missing one of the biggest opportunities God was presenting us.

But I say to you . . .

It is easy to take conventional wisdom for granted, assume its truth, and move on. After all, wisdom becomes conventional for a reason. Usually it points to enduring patterns, collective learning, and cumulative best practices. It saves us time, because we do not have to retrace the steps and relearn the lessons that previous generations have already discovered and passed down to us. But while conventional wisdom is often true, sometimes that truth has a shelf life. Reality changes, and yet we never reassess. But of course realities do change, and therefore our thinking needs to change as well. The church excels at adopting and passing along conventional wisdom without properly testing it. After all, we are entrusted with taking a centuries-old faith and passing it along to a new generation. But sometimes we confuse the faith we are passing down with methodologies, habits, and traditions that are outdated. It is these that need to be questioned, tested, and reworked.

That is especially true when it comes to planting new communities of faith that reach new people. Through the lens of conventional wisdom The Gathering made little sense. Through a new lens, it began to make perfect sense. What follows is a short case study in thinking differently. The solutions are not nearly as interesting or important as the process—questioning what the church assumes and developing new possibilities.

> **Cunningham:** In a denomination in decline, this is a critically important principle. Question our assumptions, develop new possibilities!

Our answers will not necessarily be your answers, but I hope this different way of thinking will spark you to see that God is calling you to look at your own situation differently.

From the beginning The Gathering's vision has been to create a Christian community that is compelling for new generations of people in St. Louis.

> **Brown:** Know the vision for your church the way The Gathering knows theirs.

It is no secret in United Methodism that we are failing to reach new generations with the gospel. We have been in steady decline for fifty years, a sign that we have missed at least three and maybe four generations of people. I often tell people in our congregation if you are a baby boomer or younger, you are part of a new generation the church has largely failed to reach. One way The Gathering differs is that we unapologetically put our focus on reaching new generations of people—most of whom are under the age of thirty-five.

Baughman: This is very similar to the goal of our worshipping communities at Union. At times people have criticized Union by calling it a boutique church. I am totally fine with being a boutique church. What most critics fail to see is that the majority of congregations are already boutique churches, focusing on the needs of baby boomers and older generations with a conservative-leaning theology. What they assume to be a church "for everyone" doesn't match up with the needs of those outside the demographic of their primary leadership. I don't think that one congregation needs to be a place where everyone's needs are met. There were twelve tribes of Israel—each with their own role, experience, and leadership. As long as we remember that we are all a part of the same body, I think it is a healthy thing for churches to specialize being in ministry with a particular demographic.

United Methodism consistently talks about members of younger generations who attend church as if they are unicorns, almost mythical. We believe they exist, but we never see them, at least not where we reside. There is a reason for this, and a lot of it has to do with where we have our churches.

From its launch in the fall of 2006, The Gathering was unconventional.

> **Brown:** This is expert wisdom. You have to know what makes your church different and be able to explain it.

From the style of worship to the use of resources, it didn't look like the few new churches United Methodism had started in the decade beforehand. But what was perhaps the most unconventional feature was not what it did but where it did it.

The Gathering was started in a building that until a few months prior had housed another Methodist church for over one hundred years. The building was tired and in disrepair. Nothing about it spoke "new" or "different." From the green vintage tile to the smell, it was like a thousand other churches, Methodist or otherwise, that are struggling to stay alive. Forget high-tech multimedia or state-of-the-art sound. This sanctuary didn't even have air-conditioning! Without money for the basics, its Spartan interior contrasted sharply with the modern new church plants.

But the unconventional nature of this plant didn't stop there. It was not only the building itself that differed from how most new churches begin. Located in Dogtown (an established neighborhood of St. Louis city), there were perhaps some good demographic reasons that Immanuel UMC closed after one hundred years. Since the 1950s, the city of St. Louis has been losing people to the suburbs and beyond. Signs of better days didn't stop with the overall population decline. Per capita income was down, property values struggled, and little new residential development was happening. These trends led to what was perhaps predictable and expected, the closure of several United Methodist churches in the city (not to mention churches of other denominations). Of the remaining city churches, none were growing, few were stable, and most were holding on for survival, tapping into endowments or drastically cutting mission and ministry to stay afloat. If it sounds dramatic, it was. It appeared as if the few churches left wouldn't be there for long.

Many of you reading this book will recognize the above scenario. Whether in a rural or urban setting, many of us are fighting demographics that are working against us, buildings that easily become maintenance nightmares, and people that are moving, dying, or leaving the church. It isn't easy. In the midst of such a situation, the last thing on our minds is starting something new. We are too busy trying to hold onto what we already have!

But despite the odds, I drove to my bishop's office, shared my vision, and he said yes. My conference funded it, and we started that church. Nine years later, The Gathering has four sites around St. Louis with over twelve hundred people in worship and a thriving ministry.

> **Brown:** Yay God! This is what happens when your faith is greater than your fear. Thank you, The Gathering, for trusting and believing God to achieve the impossible.

So why did the location work, and what conventional wisdom did we have to test in order to realize this vision? In our journey to start The Gathering, I bumped up against three strongly defended principles that we had to make conscious decisions to defy. It wasn't easy. In fact, many people told me I was nuts and that the plant was fatally flawed. But we prayed, listened, were willing to look at the situation differently, and by God's grace, we followed what the Spirit was prompting us to do. The solutions here are not necessarily right for every context. But this method of deep discernment, trusting in the Spirit, and a willingness to challenge conventional wisdom not only *can* be applied, but *must* be applied, in every context.

> **Cunningham:** This is important. At our next leadership meeting, we are going to spend the first half of the meeting in prayer discerning where God is leading us.

Parish Mentality

Over time, Methodism developed a parish mentality. The idea behind a parish is pretty simple: you take the geography of a particular place, divide it up, and put a church in each area whose job is to serve that particular area (or parish) exclusively. If an area grows, you divide it up further and start new churches as needed. While this makes a certain amount of sense, especially in growing areas, it doesn't work at all in established communities like St. Louis. Here's why:

St. Louis is a relatively old city, just recently celebrating its 250th birthday. The city grew rapidly in the mid to late nineteenth century and established many of the current city boundaries and features in the early twentieth century. Early Methodism was good at following the contours of growing communities and starting new churches to keep up. The trajectory of many Methodist churches followed the trajectories of their communities (per the plan). In St. Louis, nearly every existing church started sometime in the late nineteenth century and then moved around several times before settling into a permanent building sometime in the early twentieth century. When a community stops growing, we historically have stopped planting churches. We move our efforts to new places where new growth is taking place. The established communities are already covered by the existing churches. That is a parish mentality. And it is killing us.

While it sounds like a good idea on the surface, there are multiple problems with the parish approach. First, just because communities don't grow, doesn't mean they don't change. Existing churches have trouble adapting and keeping up with the changing profile of their neighborhoods. Over time, many churches fail to reach emerging generations in a neighborhood and instead survive on the continued participation of longtime members: many who no longer live in the neighborhood.

Secondly, while overall population may be in decline, the segment of people no longer attending church has grown significantly. Yet in a parish mentality, new churches are not started to reach new generations of people that have stopped going to church. In fact, we often use reverse logic: fewer people are attending church in a particular city, and we already have churches in that city; therefore, we don't need any more. Third, if a church is ineffective in reaching a neighborhood, we hire a consultant, start a new service, or appoint a new pastor. In a parish model, reforming an existing church is the only answer to ineffectiveness. Meanwhile, experience tells us reforming existing churches is a tough and long task. We also have learned that new things reach new people (think Sunday School).

Finally, all churches have a natural life cycle. They don't last forever. In a parish model, we wait until one church dies before another one is started. A wiser approach would be to have multiple churches of varying ages in a community, one that is one hundred years old, one eighty, one sixty, one forty, one twenty, and one that is new. As some churches close, new ones are already present. Churches started in various generations will have differing emphases and strengths leading to a more comprehensive and holistic approach to ministry in that neighborhood.

Despite the shortcomings of a parish mentality, in many places United Methodism has adopted a de facto parish mentality. Rather than being seen as a positive contribution to a community, new churches are viewed as competition, and turf wars break out. Surrounding pastors grow jealous or nervous, the focus remains on the people inside our churches rather than all the people yet to be reached, and we squash new possibilities before they are able to start. Too many bishops and district superintendents lack the courage or will to confront this shortsightedness, instead giving in to pressure from existing churches.

> **Baughman:** We planted in the heart of Dallas and heard the same critique from some of the larger churches in our city. They worried that our success would take young people who would otherwise attend their church, despite the fact that they had very few young people and most of our congregation is made up of people who would never set foot in a traditional church. Other, smaller congregations welcomed us into the city, knowing that we could take care of young professionals in a way they couldn't. They sometimes refer young visitors to us. Our cabinet and several nearby churches saw the "big picture" and helped us to work past the criticisms of some nearby pastors. It has been such a gift to see "kingdom-minded" partnerships develop with churches in our city and district.

In far too many places, a parish mentality keeps us from starting churches in existing communities. As a result, we are failing to reach changing neighborhoods, especially ones that are growing younger and more diverse. We exacerbate the very problems we say we want to solve. Part of the reason The Gathering worked, despite its location, is because we had failed to start new churches for the better part of one hundred years in the city of St. Louis. While we had many existing churches, they were of a similar type, of similar age, reaching a similar segment of the community. There was plenty of space for new churches with a goal of reaching new generations of people.

Today, The Gathering is one church that meets in four different locations in St. Louis. With each plant we had to overcome the parish mentality and potential resistance from other neighborhood churches. We had the benefit of a culture in our conference, led by Bishop Robert Schnase, that values growth, innovation, and church planting. This does not always exist. While we seek to be sensitive to established ministries, we simply don't believe that St. Louis can adequately be served if we do not start new ministries alongside existing ones. To date, we have started two city locations and two locations in established suburbs with other strong churches. The beginning of something new is not an indictment on current churches and their ministries. It is simply a response to the realities named above and a recognition that if we do not continue to start new ministries even in relatively strong and established suburbs of St. Louis, the decline we are experiencing in our urban core will soon be replicated in our inner ring suburbs and beyond. We must move beyond a parish mentality in all of our churches or risk suburban churches dying the same death currently experienced by urban congregations.

> **Brown:** It takes courage for denominational leaders to change a system or a way of thinking to make room for new ideas and possibilities.

Urban Neglect

The second challenge we faced is the unintended, but very real, neglect of cities in United Methodism. As a denomination, we have not focused our resources and energy on urban centers. There is some historical precedent for this—Methodism thrived as a frontier movement where circuit riders would go from place to place, nurturing leadership, raising up new small groups, and preaching. The established nature of ministry in a city made early Methodist leaders skeptical and the movement was less at home in large urban centers. In many ways, that was an early blessing. Methodism brought faith to many places that otherwise would have been neglected or ignored. Today we have a strong presence in rural communities, evidenced by the sheer number of local churches in the United States. We have a significantly weaker presence in cities.

Take St. Louis and the state of Missouri as an example. There are roughly 850 churches in the state but only 49 (6 percent) of them are in St. Louis (county and city). Meanwhile, over 20 percent of the state's population lives in that same area. We have less than 6 percent of our churches in the very place where more than 20 percent of the people live! While St. Louis is an established community with many churches, there are not nearly enough churches to reach the amount of people living there.

If we look nationwide, this trend is not unique to St. Louis. United Methodism is proportionally absent in the places where most people live. The rural and suburban focus needs to be buttressed with a new focus on urban centers. As populations shift and move, many cities are growing and many small towns that were once thriving are not. Beyond that, we have relatively few churches in the places where most people live. While it may seem like we have plenty of churches in the city, we often fail to account for just how many people live in urban areas and how many churches it would truly require in order to effectively share the gospel with them.

Even with the number of existing churches in the city, there was not much like The Gathering when it started. Couple that with the large number of people living in St. Louis, and you have the recipe for a church that can grow.

> **Cunningham:** This is affirmation of the principle: question assumptions, develop new possibilities! From my experience, the excitement and the challenge of developing a new way of being church is the experimental nature of the work. Some things work, some don't. But often, something that doesn't work so well, with some tweaking, leads to something that does work well.

More importantly, our story is about who began coming to our church. It was the very people that we talk so often about in United Methodism and yet fail to reach—young people.

One of the consequences of not focusing more effort on cities is that we miss the very people we say we want to reach. We want to reach young people but where do they live? Not in fast-growing suburbs (at least not in large numbers), but rather in the very places we often neglect.

In our area, the fast-growing suburbs on the outskirts of town are great places to plant churches, and doing so will help us reach the people who live there. But, if we want to reach people under the age of thirty-five, we have to look elsewhere. Early on I realized after poring over demographics that while the city was not growing overall, it had a very high percentage of young adults living in it, sometimes nearly double the percentage living in suburban communities.

> **Baughman:** We planted Union in a Dallas zip code with an average age of 29.5 and almost no children living nearby. I suspect that most cities have concentrated young professional populations like this.

I suspect that St. Louis is not unique. I would bet there are other urban centers (both growing and even those in decline) that would find surprising demographics on where young people live compared to where churches are planted. Such work may reveal more opportunities to plant in urban areas than was initially believed.

Sanctuaries

When The Gathering was forming in 2006, our urban district here in St. Louis was closing roughly one United Methodist church per year in the city. That summer, Immanuel United Methodist Church made the decision to close its doors. Immanuel was started in the post–Civil War era (1886) as St. Louis was experiencing its greatest growth. Initially worshipping in a home, it soon moved to a small wooden sanctuary on what was then the edge of the city. In the 1920s, they tore down the wooden structure and built a modest but impressive brick sanctuary on a large stone foundation—it was a sign that the church had matured and was here to stay. And stay it did, that is until 2006. By that time the congregation had dwindled to roughly twelve people in worship, all over the age of seventy. Finances finally dried up and decades of neglect took its toll on the building. It all caught up with them in the spring of 2006, and they reluctantly (I might add angrily) had to close their doors. The church building, as was tradition in St. Louis, was to be sold with the proceeds going to a variety of different mission ministries that the former congregation supported.

The above story is, of course, all too familiar. Whether urban, suburban, or rural, the demographics and lack of attention to invitation are catching up with us. As a denomination, we are closing, or facing the closure, of a large number of our churches. This presents an interesting question—what do we do with all those buildings? When our launch team heard about the closure of Immanuel UMC, I immediately believed this would make a great home for our new church. While there are always risks to consider when acquiring an old church building, there are also great opportunities. At the time, planting a new church in an old, established sanctuary was not en vogue. In fact, when I shared the idea of starting in an old church building, a pastor friend of mine rightly noted, "Matt, don't do it. People have been driving by and ignoring that church since the invention of the automobile." He was largely right!

We had an intuition that younger generations would appreciate historic and holy spaces. We talked with our conference leaders and convinced them to not sell that old sanctuary so that we could start The Gathering in the sanctuary. A few years into our church, we did it again and acquired another United Methodist church in our area. Clayton UMC had gone through a discernment process and realized that they wanted to reach new people in their neighborhood but did not have the people or financial resources to do so.

> **Cunningham:** It's great when you can infuse old buildings with the energy of a new faith community. We operate in a school, which has the advantage of low cost, but the disadvantage is that we have access to the space only a few hours a week.

They had roughly forty people in weekly worship and enough money to survive for another three to five years, but that was not the legacy they wanted to leave. They invited The Gathering to talk with their board. After much prayer and conversation, Clayton UMC voted to close and transfer their building and remaining assets to The Gathering. We used the remainder of their money (about $250,000) to renovate the church building. After a six-month period of inactivity, we launched the Clayton site of The Gathering in 2012. Today, there are a couple hundred people worshipping in two services at that site, and many of the former Clayton UMC members are still part of the church today.

> **Brown:** This story is awesome. Sometimes when we let go and release what we have God gives new life in ways we never expected. I have been to the Clayton worship location, and I am truly impressed by the space, hospitality, and favor of God.

Not all new churches are going to look the same, and new things don't have to ignore tradition and history. When it comes to space, not all new things have to occupy a school, a theater, or a gym. While this wisdom has changed in the nine years since we started, there is still a lingering suspicion among those who want to do something new. The Gathering found success by being an expression of faith that is historically rooted and innovatively practiced—and the building was just one example of this.

The Gathering is just one story. From the beginning, we had to question traditional wisdom and try alternative approaches to ministry. Along the way, we have helped pave a new path for ministry in St. Louis. Since our start, several other new churches have been planted in our conference in similar demographic areas using similar strategies. While the process we developed will not be right in every context, I do believe the willingness to ask different questions is always relevant.

> **Brown:** The words of wisdom Matt shares are so true. We have to think differently and try differently so we can see the power of God. As you consider planting a new church, trust God for everything.

Church Planters Have to Be Like the People They Serve

OWEN ROSS, LA FUNDICIÓN DE CRISTO MISIÓN METODISTA UNIDA

You have heard it said . . .

In 2002, I was appointed to plant Christ's Foundry United Methodist Mission. The North Texas Conference called it a "Hispanic church start." I felt insecure about the assignment. First, I had never planted a church. Second, I had never pastored a church. Third, I had never even been a part of a Hispanic congregation. Finally, I am not Hispanic. One of the most consistent lessons in church planting is to plant with your "affinity group." Despite my time spent in Latin America, it seemed unlikely that a guy like me could launch a congregation like this.

But I say to you . . .

You have heard it said that churches need to be served by indigenous leaders, but I say to you that what is required for planting

---

Owen Ross is the founding pastor of *La Fundición de Cristo Misión Metodista Unida* in Dallas, Texas. ◆ Christsfoundry.org

churches is culturally competent pastors, regardless of their indigenous affinity.

Scripture and my experience show that indigenous leadership
is not required for planting churches. Three great leaders in the
Bible have guided me in cross-cultural ministry. The House of
Pharaoh raised Moses, which meant he was culturally Egyptian
with an Israelite appearance. Paul was a Jew called to the Gentiles. Finally, the incarnation of God in Jesus Christ gave birth
to the greatest cross-cultural ministry in history, for no greater
cultural divide exists than that between heaven and earth. These
three leaders have been the model for the ministries of Christ's
Foundry, and I will use them to explore how God used a self-identi-
fied redneck, white, non-Hispanic pastor from East Texas to plant
La Fundición de Cristo Misión Metodista Unida (Christ's Foundry
United Methodist Church).

Christ's Foundry

For the past thirteen years, I have been ministering full-time with
the Spanish-speaking immigrant population living north of Love
Field in Dallas, Texas. The population within a one-mile radius
around Christ's Foundry is 33,681 in 7,194 households. Ninety percent of the population is Hispanic/Latino/a (MissionInsite 5). The
schools in this community have the highest concentration in Dallas of immigrant children who have been in the country for three
years or less. While accurate figures about unauthorized residents
are not available, many of these foreign-born residents in the north
of Love Field community are unauthorized to reside in the United
States. Moreover, the per capita income of the community is *two-
fifths* the national average.[1]

For years, church judicatories have been closing churches in
such neighborhoods, yet Christ's Foundry has flourished. After
thirteen years, Christ's Foundry touches over three thousand lives

each year. The average attendance in worship is 230, and midweek small group attendance is over 150. Our social services touch hundreds more each week. The ministries of Christ's Foundry reflect the community, with 98 percent of the participants being Latin American immigrants or children of Latin American immigrants.

Moses: Speaking to power, leading the oppressed, struggling to speak

Throughout my thirteen years in ministry, I have identified with Moses's cross-cultural struggles. Moses was born during a time when the government had ordered the death of all boys born to the Hebrews. Like many immigrants today who send their children across waters to an uncertain future instead of facing certain persecution, Moses's mother floated her son down the Nile River to an uncertain future in a basket made of grass. Moses was found by Pharaoh's daughter and was raised as her son in the house of Pharaoh. A Hebrew by birth, Moses became an Egyptian by culture.

As an adult, Moses had an identity crisis in witnessing the mistreatment of the Hebrews and how hard his biological brothers worked. In a crime of passion, Moses killed an Egyptian that was beating a Hebrew, leading Moses to flee Egypt. While tending sheep in the wilderness far from Egypt, God called Moses: "I am sending you to Pharaoh to bring my people the Israelites out of Egypt" (Ex. 3:10). God was sending Moses to face the powerful Pharaoh, and also to lead the oppressed Israelites—he had a foot in both of these worlds.

Moses responded to God, "Who am I that I should go to Pharaoh and bring the Israelites out of Egypt?" (Ex. 3:11). Upon my graduation from seminary, I felt much more confident going to powerful people than planting a church among a community of largely undocumented Latino/a immigrants. That was intimidating! My seminary experience prepared me to talk *about* the poor rather than to talk *with* them.

Baughman: When I graduated from seminary, I believed that the ability to think theologically about something meant that I knew how to do that something. While the ability to reflect theologically on the practice of ministry *is critical* to faithfully executing ministry, it does not always lead to skills in accomplishing ministry work. For example, seminary taught me how to think theologically about money and giving. It did not teach me how to actually raise money—which is kind of important for pastors who lead organizations that are funded primarily by donations.

Perhaps Moses felt the same way.

Because of my comfort in speaking to wealthier, more powerful people, I spent a lot of my early years in the ministry of Christ's Foundry building support among more affluent churches. Not only was I more comfortable there, I also was aware that long-term financial support would be needed for holistic ministries in this community. As our ministry has unfolded, these relationships with wealthier congregations have been essential to the financial well-being of Christ's Foundry.

While my path has been similar to Moses's in some ways, in other ways I chose another approach. For example, God put worship at the center of Moses's initial calling. God said to Moses, "I will be with you. And this will be the sign to you that it is I who have sent you: When you have brought the people out of Egypt, you will worship God on this mountain" (Ex. 3:12). I had heard from others that I should start to build trust by initially establishing social services. I found getting people to participate in social services is easier than getting them involved in worship services.

Therefore, rather than putting worship at the center of the calling, social service served as the initial focus.

Contrary to this bit of church wisdom, however, I discovered that beneficiaries of the social services often see adding worship services after establishing social services as a bait and switch scheme. Becoming a worshipping community requires a fundamental switch when the organization has already established social services DNA. Moreover, starting with social services independent of worship establishes a relationship that reflects the world's haves-versus-have-nots structure, the divide between superior and inferior, providers and recipients. Such services position the church planter as someone serving the people without becoming a part of the people. Fourteen years later, Christ's Foundry is still dealing with my error of beginning with social services.

> **Baughman:** I am so grateful to Owen's insight on this point. He served as a guide for me when I was strongly encouraged to delay launching a worship gathering until we had built significant credibility in our community. His advice to launch a worshipping community within six months of opening our doors proved invaluable and has bolstered our credibility with people who do not like the church, but are appreciative that we have been straightforward about who we are even though we run a coffee shop.

In another way, I did follow Moses. While studying church planting at Africa University in Zimbabwe as part of my seminary education, Professor John Kurewa told the class, "When going to plant a church, first go get permission from the chief. The chief may never come to your church, but he can sure help you or stop you." Similarly, God told Moses, "Go, assemble the elders of Israel" (Ex. 3:16).

In certain cultures, identifying the chiefs and elders is easier than in others. In the North Field neighborhood, the schools had clout. While some people I met through the schools have come to Christ's Foundry, my activity in the schools primarily served to give me standing in the community as I was beginning.

I related to Moses in one more way as he pled with God, "I am slow of speech and tongue" (Ex. 4:10). I remember realizing I had never in all of my Spanish-language training and experience learned the word for *mercy*. Our beginning was slow and my learning curve with language as well as culture was big. I have wondered if Moses was insecure about his fluency in the slaves' language.

> **Baughman:** That's brilliant insight!

God explains to Moses that God will help him speak, will teach him what to say, and will send Moses's brother to help him communicate. God has sent many people to me along my journey to grow my cultural competencies and to assist me in the planting of Christ's Foundry. Culturally competent companions are essential in equipping others to be culturally competent. I thank God for those teachers and experiences that God has put in my life that have enabled me to be in ministry with the people of Christ's Foundry.

Paul: Being self-aware, adapting to context, transforming "me" into "us"

Moses taught me to get over the message that I would be ineffective at ministry with people unlike myself. Paul has assisted me in learning *how* to be in ministry with people from a culture other than that of my upbringing. Of his own cross-cultural ministry,

Paul wrote, "I have become all things to all people so that by all possible means I might save some" (1 Cor. 9:22). In that chapter, Paul explains the cultural competency involved in his ministry. Paul sought to become like those he sought to win for the Kingdom.

Paul did not pretend he was something he was not. Paul repeatedly identified himself as a Jew (Acts 19:34, 21:39). Church planters in a cross-cultural setting must be aware of their own ancestry, racial appearance, and identity, yet at the same time seek to make the story of those they serve their own story. Cultural competency assists in transforming a *me/them* relationship into an *us*.

Rangel: The same issue happened to me when I became the senior pastor at Casa Linda in 2012. As a young, Spanish-speaking minister that came to the United States I had to learn the culture of the Anglo members of the church. In order for the transition to go smoothly I paid very close attention to such things as the length of service, the liturgy in worship, the dress code of the minister, and the importance of the adult Sunday school. All these were not relevant to my style or the Spanish-speaking congregation, however it was important to the original congregation. These were a few things I had to consider in order to minister to them in their own context while at the same time meeting the ministry needs of the Spanish-speaking group.

While I never identify myself as Hispanic/Latino, when talking about the struggle of a people, I tend to use first person plural pronouns. *Their* sufferings are *my* suffering. *Their* joys are *my* joys, thus becoming *our* sufferings and joys. In sharing life together with the people of Christ's Foundry, my cultural competency has grown. God erodes the divisions between *them* and *me*, and we continually grow into becoming *us*.

Paul clearly understood the importance of culture in building relationships and in communicating the gospel message. In Romans 14 and 1 Corinthians 8, Paul is aware that cultural norms associated with diet could affect the communication of the gospel. In Acts 17, Paul uses the altar to an unknown god in Athens as a cultural symbol to communicate the gospel. Paul repeatedly showed his cultural competency in his contextualization of the gospel message.

Food and cultural symbols have very much been a part of the success of Christ's Foundry. I am thankful for parents who made me "clean my plate" at meals. I learned to eat food that I did not particularly like. While God had to tell Peter three times to eat the Gentile's food in Acts 10, my openness to unfamiliar food has enabled me to dine with people of different cultures. Even Jesus told the disciples, "Eat what is offered to you" (Luke 10:8). Gathering around food has been an essential part of the planting and growing of Christ's Foundry. Our most successful small groups by no coincidence have the best meals.

On each Sunday, Christ's Foundry includes Holy Communion in our worship and a meal following the service. Congregants prepare the meal after service. The food is sold, with half of the profit going to a ministry or a personal need and the other half going in the general budget of the church. This ministry adds to the fellowship of the church, assists in individual and ministry needs, while financially contributing to the church's work.

In 2014, I wanted to have a private breakfast for our high school graduates and their families before the worship service, something we had done in my childhood church. I sought to organize it and put some of the mothers of the graduates in charge of the meal. Next thing I know, these mothers had organized a lunch *for the entire congregation*. When I asked what happened, they responded, "It seems ugly for us to eat upstairs without everyone." This comment took me back to my Peace Corps days in Ecuador, when I discovered the hard way how rude it was to purchase something to eat or drink without purchasing something for everyone in our group. Clearly, everyone makes mistakes in ministry, and cross-cultural ministry settings will be full of such errors.

When I first began knocking on doors, I assumed a polo shirt and khaki pants would be the appropriate dress. Few would open their doors to me on my first outing. I soon realized that wearing a border-patrol green polo was not the best cultural symbol to promote in an immigrant neighborhood. I began to wear a clerical collar any time I am in the church or the community.

> **Rangel:** For Owen wearing a clerical collar or clerical robe might have worked out fine but in my context it did not. Some of the Spanish-speaking members, especially those who came from the Roman Catholic Church, found it confusing. In some cases the Hispanic Latino new believers in the United States, just as Owen states below, are very much anti-Catholic and want to steer away from anything to do with the Roman Catholic Church. In my context this would not benefit my ministry.

A police officer has an easier time stopping traffic when in a police uniform. Likewise, doors have opened and I have been able to have conversations with strangers while wearing a collar.

Although I did adopt the clerical collar, I usually avoid wearing a black shirt, because I want to differentiate myself from Roman Catholic priests. Religious prejudices tend to be strong in the Latino/a context. A friend of mine once noted, "There seems to be two churches in the Hispanic community: the Catholic Church and the anti-Catholic church." In many ways, my friend is correct. Our local Roman Catholic Church would pass out cards for their members to put on their doors: "This is a Catholic home. We do not wish to receive propaganda from any sect." Then, once I knocked on the home of a Pentecostal man who said to me, "I am sure glad you are out here to save these Catholics." As a granddaughter of the Roman Catholic Church and the mother of the Pentecostals (the "anti-Catholics"), The United Methodist Church has a unique role to play in this religiously charged context that divides families and communities.

Christ's Foundry seeks to use the best of these two religious cultures in our worship service. Communion is served each Sunday following a traditional liturgy, which is similar to Roman Catholic worship. On the other hand, the pastor wears a clerical collar and jeans. The almost Catholic-sounding liturgy is followed by music, preaching, and prayer styles that would be found in the Pentecostal/Evangelical churches. To the Roman Catholics, I became like a Roman Catholic. To the Pentecostals and Evangelicals, I became like a Pentecostal/Evangelical "so that by all possible means I might save some" (1 Cor. 9:19-22), and many have been saved.

Jesus: Learning cultures, crossing boundaries, making disciples of all nations

The primary model for my ministry is Jesus. "Now Jesus himself was about thirty years old when he began his ministry" (Luke 3:23). Viv Grigg in *Companion to the Poor* asserts that Jesus waited thirty years before beginning his ministry in order to learn the Aramaic and Jewish culture.[2] Beyond learning the Aramaic and Jewish culture, I argue that Jesus—who came from heaven— was also learning the culture of earth, crossing the greatest of all cultural divides. This argument that Jesus was a student of the culture before becoming a transformer of the culture suggests those who follow him today should follow his model and become culturally competent. While the population of Jesus's context was less diverse than today's in the United States, Jesus travelled internationally and lived in one of the more diverse areas of the world. Jesus's response to encounters with people from outside of the culture of his upbringing can assist the church planter in cross-cultural ministries.

I was an adult before I was immersed into a Latino/a culture. No one in my family of origin speaks Spanish. Very few Hispanics resided in my hometown of Henderson, Texas. However, at age twenty, after my sophomore year in college, I spent two months in Puebla, Mexico, studying Spanish. I returned and changed my primary major to International Studies with a focus on Latin America. I began studying Latin American culture, politics, and Spanish. I spent time in Latin America, including two years as a United States Peace Corps Volunteer in Ecuador. When I returned to the United States to begin seminary, I had spent more time in Latin America over the previous five years than inside the United States. In seminary, I studied Latin American theologies; took trips to Mexico, Honduras, Cuba, and Ecuador; and studied in El Salvador.

My time traveling and living with families in Latin America changed me. While I still had a white non-Hispanic appearance and ancestry, my culture had changed. Aspects of a person's life that are typically used to identify a culture tended for me to be more Hispanic/Latino/a than non-Hispanic/Latino/a. Through these experiences, God was preparing me for ministry in Christ's Foundry.

In spite of God's efforts to prepare me, I made mistakes. When I first started knocking on doors in the Christ's Foundry community, I started with the question, "What are the needs of the community?" In hindsight, I should have started with the question, "Will you help me?"

Baughman: This is another insight that has been incredibly helpful to me at Union. I used to be hesitant to ask people for help. I thought it communicated weakness and knew it would mean I'd have less control of the outcome. What I have learned is that asking for help honors the other person, makes them want to be a part of the ministry. Also, it does mean that I lose control, but so long as it advances Union's mission, turning control over to community members is a great thing.

A needs-based approach diminishes the assets of the community, because it assumes they have nothing to offer. Jesus's first experience outside the culture of his birth family was his family's receiving some men "from the east" who brought Jesus gifts (Matt. 2:1-12). When planting in a cross-cultural context, the planter must be ready to receive and utilize the gifts that the people and the culture of the community have to offer.

Rangel: In previous decades Casa Linda, similar to Christ's Foundry, focused on running community programs. People from the community referred to Casa Linda as "the church with money," even though that was not the case. It was the picture we represented for them. In recent years we have worked hard to help our community see us as a church rather than a community center. To bring about this change, we always had a staff person or church members attend the program and welcome everyone while sharing information about the church. These persons also stayed and talked one-on-one with people about their lives and how the church could be helpful for them. We use the community programs to connect the people from the community with the resource but also to be strategic in never letting them leave without connecting them to the church in some way.

As I relinquished more and more control of the ministry, the congregation and ministries grew. For example, in 2008 a woman in our community, María, had three brain surgeries, and her fourteen-year-old son was diagnosed with cancer. María began receiving food assistance from First United Methodist Church of Dallas. A year later, she had healed from her surgeries, and her son was declared cancer free. Her caseworker suggested that she begin a food assistance program at Christ's Foundry to help more people. María has now grown the feeding ministry and provides food for over four hundred people a month in Christ's Foundry. My role in this was simply to accept the gifts that María and others had to offer and to support them.

Jesus's second documented cross-cultural encounter took place when his family illegally crossed out of Judea at night and fled to Egypt. As Jesus's family traveled and settled in Egypt and then later traveled and settled in Nazareth, Galilee, surely the family would have received gifts of hospitality in their journeys. Unfortunately, no information exists about Jesus's experiences in Egypt or his settling in Nazareth, but it is likely that in these experiences Jesus was developing the cross-cultural competencies required of refugee, migrant, and immigrant children.

In beginning his ministry at age thirty, Jesus proclaimed that his ministry would reach beyond his home culture. After spending some time away from Nazareth, he returned to Nazareth in order to share his calling with his home synagogue (Luke 4). After sharing the news of his calling, Jesus added that Elijah had been sent to minister "to a widow in Zarephath in the region of Sidon" and Elisha had been sent to a Syrian (Luke 4:25b-27). Jesus would live out this calling beyond the culture of his birth in his ministry with Roman centurions, a Phoenician woman, and Samaritans as well as with Jews from various subcultures.

Christ's Foundry is already reaching out to non-Hispanics. This past year, we converted one of our Spanish services into a bilingual service. The service is designed for the monolingual English or monolingual Spanish speaker.

Baughman: It seems to me that Christ's Foundry is reflecting its name. The Foundry in the early Methodist movement was a site where the leadership (well-educated men like John Wesley) was able to work together with people of radically different backgrounds to care for the poor and advance the gospel.

While attendance at the Spanish service has plateaued, the bilingual service has doubled. This service is growing because children of Spanish-speaking immigrants and their children prefer English. We are also seeing mixed families and non-Hispanic people in this bilingual service.

Rangel: This is Casa Linda's current challenge: how can we make sure the future generation is being ministered to in their own English language? Christ Foundry's idea of opening a bilingual service has given me an option to consider for ministering to those who prefer English.

Jesus commissioned the disciples in Matthew 28 and in Acts 1 into ministry that went beyond their own nation and cultures. Christ's Foundry continues to grow in this area. Still, on any given Sunday, Christ's Foundry has six to eight countries represented. Food, fellowship, music, and most of all, the gospel of Jesus Christ keeps us together.

Love

From 2002 to 2005, I was a part of a candidacy group for ordination in The United Methodist Church. Although I was the only one ministering in a Hispanic context, the group was interested in the subject of non-Hispanics ministering to Hispanics. The group invited Pastor Guy Jones, chaplain of the Lydia Patterson Institute in El Paso, Texas, to speak to our group. Pastor Guy, as the students knew him, is white and non-Hispanic but ministered in a Hispanic/Latino/a context. Pastor Guy was flown from El Paso to Dallas. He was put up at a hotel and was given a small stipend. Some of my peers drove almost two hundred miles to meet Pastor Guy in Dallas. We were all ears and eager for the deep wisdom that this veteran of Hispanic ministries would bestow on all of us.

I posed the question to Pastor Guy, "So how do we as non-Hispanics minister to the Hispanic population?" Pastor Guy responded, "You just got to love 'em." Awkward silence followed. We, as a group preparing for ordination and service in the church in Texas, needed more.

When the question was posed once again to Pastor Guy, we pretty much received the same response. "I have found if you love them and they know you love them, then you will be effective at ministering with them," Pastor Guy frankly shared. I do not remember what else Pastor Guy said, however, the need to love the people and ensure that they know that they are loved has stayed with me.

Undoubtedly, loving people includes seeking to learn their culture. Moses eventually quit making excuses, went back to his father-in-law, and said, "Let me return to *my own people* in Egypt" (Ex. 4:18, emphasis mine). God knocked Paul off of his horse and sent him to the Gentiles. Today Jesus continues to call the church's attention to neglected populations. Cultural competency can be taught, and Jesus has redefined for us who are our *own people*.

> **Rangel:** I wish we did a better job, as a denomination, providing the correct training for pastors to be more culturally competent. This could allow pastors to serve congregations that are not the same ethnicity or language as theirs. Before serving at Casa Linda, I took a class on diversity that helped me be more competent among the diverse cultures that represent Casa Linda.

You have heard it said that churches needed to be led by indigenous leadership, but I say to you that the church needs to quit making excuses and love people who are not like them.

Churches Can't Bring in the "New" without Losing the "Old"

DAVID RANGEL, CASA LINDA UNITED METHODIST CHURCH

You have heard it said . . .

With actions, if not words, many church members communicate that they just want to belong to a church that includes people who share their interests and who look, speak, and do church the way they do. Casa Linda United Methodist Church was a middle-class Anglo congregation founded in the 1950s. Despite the Spanish name (derived from the neighborhood) the members of the church were English speakers. For roughly fifty years, Casa Linda (Pretty House) reflected the demographics of its founding congregation and "did church" in the following way:

- Its members spoke only English.
- The church was organized by committees for everything.
- Though there were multiple services, worship was traditional and in English.

David Rangel is the pastor of Casa Linda United Methodist Church in Dallas, Texas. ◆ casalinda.org

- The church held community events but there was no strategic plan to connect those people with the life of the church.
- Mission was practiced through events and trips.
- The primary means for discipleship were women's group, men's group, and strong Sunday school classes.
- The church was more inwardly than outwardly focused.

There would be nothing wrong with this church if we were still in the 1950s. In 2004 the church was in a transitional stage, dominated by a maintenance mode mentality. On average, members were elderly. There were no new people and no diversity, despite significant demographic change in the surrounding neighborhood. Casa Linda's membership was decreasing to a point where the church could have closed. The current demographics of the United States—full of people of different cultures and languages—present a challenge for churches that have been in existence for over fifty years. Many churches are faced with a choice: die slowly or transition into something they have not been before. In order to survive, the congregation I served needed to not just change but also *want* to change.

> **Baughman:** This is the critical point facing so many churches. The more congregations that choose to die slowly, the more resources are being squandered that could be used for revitalization and transformation. That said, David is absolutely right. The congregation has to want to change if they are going to ever truly invest in transformation. That may be the greatest challenge that pastors like David face.

But I say to you . . . why not?

Casa Linda is now a church where people of diverse languages, colors, nationalities, and ages are part of who we are. This transition brought a bilingual and diverse membership that includes young immigrant families worshipping alongside English-speaking members. The original church opened its doors to a new ministry intent on reaching out to the Hispanic/Latino community. The purpose of this new church plant was accomplished, but becoming one congregation was the new challenge. The church has become a place where the older people have embraced the new ones and together are moving forward to create opportunities to make disciples. The way we "do church" is not the same as it was in the '50s but more relevant to our community and members. This was not easy, and it required change.

1. We do not have "committees for everything." Instead we have strategic, temporary teams that coordinate a one-time event or program and then dissolve. We continue having a lay leadership team that nominates people for leadership roles. There is one church council that makes sure we accomplish the mission of the local church and deals with building, finance, staff, membership, and church matters. All these teams are aligned to fulfill the mission of the local church and allow the people to be busy in ministry rather than meetings.

2. We no longer base everything around programs (because that is what we had always done) but on the mission of the church: *Embrace people with the love of Jesus; empower them to grow into spiritual maturity; and equip them to find their place of service in God's world.* This means that all programs, events, and projects—whether they are new or old—must fulfill the mission of the local church.

3. We are an outwardly/inwardly focused church. We engage intentionally with the community and constantly challenge the members to reach out to others. At the same time, we nurture the current members.

4. The temporary teams, nominating committee, and church council include both Spanish and English speakers of diverse ages.

Baughman: This is such a critical point. Leadership has to reflect the target demographics for ministry with more than just token representation.

---

5. The church used to have two English worship services (traditional and blended) and one in Spanish. The English worship services had no connection with the Spanish service. Now we have two worship services: one traditional English service and one Spanish contemporary service with earphone translation in English. Whoever brings the message preaches in both services, and the praise band is formed by both English and Spanish speakers.

Cunningham: Wow! This is a powerful crossing of the boundary of language! Sounds like Acts 2:4. My church is limited in this regard by my lack of ability to speak Spanish. We have one worship service. English is the primary language, but we have lay leaders who lead songs, pray, lead communion, and read the scripture in English and Spanish. The sermon is in English with Spanish translation available by headphones.

---

6. Instead of having youth and children's ministry for the English and another for the Spanish group, there is only one bilingual youth and one bilingual children's ministry.

> **Cunningham:** The teaching of Jesus that in order to enter the Way of God we must become like children is true in so many ways. The natural ability of children to pick up language makes them natural leaders in building boundary-crossing community.

7. Instead of having more worship services throughout the week and special services during the month, we focus on small groups. This change connects the existing members and brings in new ones.

By educating the congregation, we were able to inspire a willingness to change. People might be open and willing, but lack of information and communication will make the change scary. To address this, we made sure to communicate not just *what* was to be changed, but also *why* the change was needed. This "why change" message was transmitted through town hall meetings, social media, brief Sunday announcements, teachings, sermons, written reports or updates, and any other way we could find.

One-time communication is not enough. Another important point is to communicate the change by supporting it with evidence. The use of statistics, interviews, demographics reports, and other specific information about the current situation of the church as well as our hopes for the results of the transition benefitted our work. Church members need a vision for how ministry can improve, not just a list of what is wrong.

Pastoral staff played a critical role in helping Casa Linda navigate through a demographic expansion. My predecessor, Rev. James Minor, came with the vision of a diverse church, a church that could reach out to people who might look different from the current members. He knew the church was in a transitional neighborhood and believed something had to be done. His guidance in the first years of his appointment shaped the church and prepared for a new diverse ministry. By the time I was appointed as the associate to develop Spanish ministry and grow a new Spanish-speaking church in 2008, the English-speaking older members were open to reaching out and willing to invest in Spanish-speaking ministry. Minor and I never gave up encouraging and educating the church about how to be one diverse congregation. When Reverend Minor presented the vision of the "new one church" to the church council, I stood alongside him and was involved throughout the process of transitioning to one church. When I became appointed as pastor for the unified church in 2012, the leadership team simply continued supporting the vision that had carried us so far. Because we were both involved in working with core leadership, the transition to one church was successful.

I believe that churches in a transition stage like Casa Linda need a pastor who can attract a diverse group to the church and carry the vision of a new kind of church to them. Transitioning congregations need a senior pastor and an associate (the pastor of the new ministry) to share the same vision and to be willing to learn how to work together in the midst of the cultural diversity, especially if they do not share the same cultural background.

As the associate (and then as the senior) pastor, this approach made me expand my call from only Spanish ministry to a diverse bilingual and cultural ministry. In order to make this a smooth transition, I had to learn the culture of the original church. Seemingly small things such as the length of the service, liturgy in worship, dress code of the minister, and the importance of the adult Sunday school were not relevant to my style or the Spanish speaking group. I needed to consider these things in order to minister to the original church in their own context while ministering to the Spanish speaking group. All this provided me with an open vision and experience of what is needed for a church that wants to begin a new ministry that reaches new demographic groups.

Of course for the pastors and congregation this new approach of "doing church" was different. In our case, the obstacles and challenges we faced were these:

- *Fear of making changes.* Fear can become a huge obstacle for the church to reach its goals toward transition. The biggest obstacle is always fear of the unknown.
- *Cultural difference.* Cultural miscommunication can undermine both the existing and new ministries. These differences, if the church does not explore and accept them, then become an issue. We discovered the following cultural differences between the English-speaking and Spanish-speaking members.
  a. Punctuality: one group is always on time; the other, not so much.
  b. Worship: for one group worship is solemn; for the other; it needs to be experiential and expressive. For the latter group, time is not an issue.
  c. Building usage: everybody uses the same space, but one group was used to putting things back the way they were, while for the other group leaving things out was normal. Our biggest battle was the kitchen. A formal agreement had to be made and posted.
  d. Meetings: for one group, committees and meetings are normal; and for the other, this is abnormal.
  e. Religious affinity: for one group the clerical robe and sanctuary items could be meaningful elements of worship, while for the other group, they represent their old religion (Catholicism). In some cases for the Hispanic/Latino new believers in the United States, this can be confusing. (To avoid this I suggest educating the people in the significance of liturgical items.)

- *Inclusive language.* Approaching the old and new members using "your church, your congregation, your stuff, or your people" would not develop a sense of unity and inclusiveness. "We" and "our" became increasingly important pronouns to use.
- *Power dynamics.* New people felt ignored and devalued when the long-tenured members made decisions. Concentrating power with one group or the other could isolate the others instead of moving together as one body in Christ.
- *Risking loss.* At the beginning of the process, we lost a few members who did not support the vision of one diverse church. Over time, however, we gained a lot of new members.
- *Building space.* The fact that the doors would be open for a new group of people was not an easy thing. It took time for the existing church to feel the confidence that the rooms and space would be well cared for. On some occasions the old members needed to agree to share or give up a room for a new class for the new people.
- *Programming versus discipleship.* We stopped doing programs just because the church was used to doing them for many years and began to focus on discipleship. In other words, we discovered that there were some programs that were relevant decades ago but not today. Besides this, some of the programs were done because they were part of the annual calendar. The church agreed to end programs that were not making disciples or were poorly aligned to the mission, but to leave and add programs that fulfill these two factors. The true need was to guide a new believer to become a faithful servant and disciple of Christ. Kaleb Rangel, the associate pastor, and I created a discipleship track called Ruta 180 (Route 180), a six-month-long ministry, designed to take a new believer through a life-changing experience, a 180-degree turn.

> **Cunningham:** This sounds like the call of Jesus in Mark 1:15-20, repent and believe. Make a 180-degree turn and become those who fish for other new believers.

The program involves the following courses and retreats:

    f. *Genesis*: course with principles to begin a relationship with God.

    g. *Grow*: course with practical information to grow in relationship with God.

    h. *Experience*: retreat in which the grace of God is manifested in a personal way.

    i. *D 1 to 1*: course to make disciples one-on-one.

    j. *Renew:* retreat that renews the spirit in commitment to God.

    k. *Fundamentals*: course that solidifies the relationship with God, which is the basis for Christian life.

The purpose of Ruta 180 ministry is to equip new believers to make new disciples. The growth of the Spanish ministry at Casa Linda is due largely to this ministry.

- *Decision making and planning.* Most of the Spanish first-generation immigrants are not used to being in committees and meetings. The reality is that the church would need representation from those who crave meetings and those who could easily do without them. A well-balanced meeting agenda can make meetings work for both groups.

- *Finances.* In a new Hispanic/Latino church, inspiring donations can be a challenge. The issue is not that they do not have money to give but that a new believer of any culture requires the right teaching about stewardship in order to learn practices of giving. When developing a plan to incorporate new believers of any ethnicity into the life of the church, the financial plan will need to include time for the new people to commit themselves to giving on a regular basis.

- *Building versus ministry.* For one group, ministry was about keeping the building clean and paying bills, while for the other group it was about bringing people to Christ and into the building. The more new people visit the church, the messier it will be. To find a balance between maintaining the building and using the building to bring new people in takes a lot of effort and understanding between the old and new members.

- *Unity.* Learning to worship together or share fellowship as one church was not easy. People would go and sit with their own people or with those who speak the same language. They, understandably, chose worship services that more closely matched their cultural context. It has taken a long time to develop a pattern of worshipping together. Even today when we worship together every fifth Sunday of the month, a few people decide not to attend that day because they struggle with the worship experience.

Besides the obstacles and challenges, we also faced opposition. Newton's third law of motion applies to churches as well, it seems: *For every action, there is an equal and opposite reaction.*

Baughman: There's a lot of wisdom in this—especially for established congregations. That said, I've seen this happen with new church starts as well. It only takes one year to build a "tradition" in which people might find ways to resist as a new church start continues to innovate and create new practices from year to year.

When it comes to taking actions that cause change, then reactions, resistance, and opposition appear. There is nothing wrong with reactions, resistance, and opposition. What would be wrong is letting these issues control and manipulate the change.

At Casa Linda we intentionally created opportunities to reduce the impact of these reactions. We began leading activities or events where diverse people could interact and get to know each other. We worshipped together every fifth Sunday, Christmas, anniversary Sunday, and Easter. We included both old and new members in leading those worship services or special events. Another way was to involve old and new members in committees and teams. Both pastors participated in worship in some capacity, and both were involved in pastoral care situations, so each minister was able to counsel, visit, or help members of the other ethnicity. In other words, all pastors and staff ministered to the entire church.

For a transitional church it will be helpful to have a visioning team of laypeople that can discern the changes that need to be made and where the church should go. This way, all of the decisions and recommendations are not coming from the clergy alone. This team studies demographic information and ministry insight alongside the pastor. Involving laypeople in the process gives greater "buy-in" to the process.

When an established Anglo congregation is starting a ministry with new people from a different demographic, it is important that both demographics be seen for the value they add to the new way forward. In our context, the new ministry was intended to keep the existing church alive and then help it transition into something new. I knew about the financial situation the church was facing, and how the need to repair and maintain an old building could hinder a new ministry. The new ministry had no option but to grow and help the existing church survive. Hence the challenge was not only to grow the new ministry but at the same time help the new ministry connect intentionally with the existing church, so the two could become one church.

It is not easy to be a planter in a transitional church. As a planter I had to learn how the existing church practiced ministry in the previous years as well as what moved them in ministry. I had to discover their vision, mission, and core values not only on paper but also as they were lived out. I learned the importance of "negotiation." I had to discover what the existing church did not want to lose and what they would be willing to give up in order to understand the best way to "do church" in a transitional ministry. If the existing church is not the same ethnicity as you are, then expect cultural challenges.

Just as it was important for the Anglo congregation to learn about Hispanic culture and for me to learn about the existing church culture, it was important that the new congregation members intentionally learn the culture of the existing church. The pastor cannot serve as the only bridge, nor is all the responsibility on the preexisting congregation.

Cunningham: This is such an important principle—the pastor facilitates and inspires ministry rather than trying to do it all! We have just started a ministry where twelve leaders are responsible for leading small groups and pastoring to the people in their groups. We meet once a month to evaluate our experiences and think together about how to improve our pastoral work. It is also having a transforming impact on those leaders and in the congregation.

Sometimes these multicultural interactions can be comical. I will never forget when our office volunteer picked up a call, then came to my office and knocked on my door, and said, "Pastor David, you have a phone call."

"Who is it?" I asked.

She responded, "It's a man, and he said his name is Jesus." (Jesus is a very common name in the Spanish community.) She added, "You may be in big trouble for Jesus himself to call you." We both laughed, and then I spoke to Jesus. To be in a transitional church is to adapt yourself to names and customs, and to learn to laugh at these adaptation moments.

I see the following thirteen conditions as critical for successfully transitioning a congregation into a new, multicultural identity:

1. A transitional neighborhood;
2. Existing members willing to make changes in order to become a new diverse congregation;

> **Cunningham:** This is so important. In building a boundary-crossing congregation, it has been critical for us to find and work with people who have a passion for crossing social boundaries.

3. The right planter with cultural affinity toward both the mission field and the existing church;
4. Staff and leaders (senior pastor, associates, directors, and leaders) with the same vision who are trained in transitional ministry;
5. Multicultural lay teams/committees and bilingual staff;
6. An intentional discipleship and equipping program;
7. Prayer team supporting the church before, during, and after the transition;
8. Effective communication, and intentional inclusive language;

> **Cunningham:** We have struggled with this for years. It's been important to empower lay leaders who can pray, read, sing, and speak fluently in English and Spanish.

9. A good building;
10. Visioning team;

11. Financial stability and preferably no debt;
12. Workshops related to diversity, hospitality, worship, mission-vision, building usage, and the like;
13. Intentional worship services and fellowship including the old and new members.

The early church had to face a transitional stage. In Acts 2 God did not help the crowd to understand the message in Greek or Hebrew but performed a miracle: the gospel was proclaimed in each listener's own language. About three thousand people were added to the church that day. There will not be white, Hispanic, African, or Asian sections in heaven; we will all be one.

If we look at our surroundings perhaps we will see diversity and new people who do not know about Christ, and perhaps we will see a repetition of the miracle in Acts 2. I do not promise that your church will grow to three thousand people, but maybe some people will be added to your church. We have the great opportunity to share the gospel with them, and invite them to be not like us but like Jesus.

In a transitional church I do not become like you, and you do not become like me. We all become like Jesus.

Baughman: This is beautiful. This should be the model for all of our ministries.

Churches Don't Grow in the Summer

OLU BROWN, IMPACT CHURCH

Planting a new church is a blessing and a burden. If you have heard this saying, let me confirm it is true. I am a church planter who, with twenty-five people, launched out on a vision more than five years ago to start a new faith community near downtown Atlanta named Impact Church. Today, Impact is one of the fastest-growing United Methodist churches in the United States and the second-largest in attendance in the North Georgia Annual Conference. I don't often rattle off these stats, but I believe they are worth citing, because they let you know that my guidance to you has been tested and proven to work. At the same time, I cannot claim to know everything there is to know about sustaining a vibrant faith community—even through summer months. Still, our team of volunteers and staff constantly seeks out information related to growing a healthier congregation. We constantly tweak our systems for greater effectiveness and to enhance growth in volunteers, attendance, and generosity for our local church.

Olu Brown is the founding pastor for Impact Church in Atlanta, Georgia. ◆ Impactdoingchurchdifferently.org

You have heard it said . . .

Over the past few years we have learned a lot about gathering people, building teams, and the real truth of church planting: "after Sunday comes Sunday." I wish I had taken this wisdom more seriously when we first planted, but I was too focused on other things like a quality sound system, butts in seats, and email blasts. Now, as we prepare to launch our second campus, we are better positioned and in a wiser frame of mind to launch with the understanding that "after Sunday comes Sunday." If you are scratching your head, wondering what this statement means, it simply means that when we wake up from the awesome church "hangover" on Mondays we realize, "Oh my God, Sunday is coming again in a few days!"

This weekly dynamic will soon become routine, and once you get into the swing of Sundays, you will have another panic-filled revelation, somewhere around spring. You will wake up one morning realizing that summer is around the corner. Church planters and existing church pastors alike dread the summer, because congregants frequently leave town for vacations or simply take a break from regular church attendance. This is the catalyst to the summer curse. As a result:

1. Volunteer rosters sink like boulders in the ocean because there are fewer people to support volunteer stations.
2. Giving decreases because many of the people who give regularly nine months out of the year may be away during the summer, and if your church doesn't support electronic giving they may not be present to give.
3. Overall attendance takes a nosedive because attendance equals people and people equals attendance.

Perhaps we need a new motto: "After Easter comes summer." In order to grow in the summer months, each church must plan for success in the summer. We assume that no church planter is ever able to outmaneuver or outsmart the power of "Almighty Summer." We have become accustomed to summer declines in attendance and giving as families, neighborhoods, and communities ebb and flow. We are so accustomed to this phenomenon that we consider it natural.

If this phenomenon is familiar to you, you may be a church planter about to experience the summer jitters or an existing church pastor holding on just to make it through the warmest months of the year. Remember, the catalyst to the summer curse is members of the congregation taking vacations or deciding to take a break from regular church attendance during the summer, which means a catastrophic loss of people and resources at a new church. Believe me; the concern is real. That said, we should not consider summer decline to be a natural phenomenon nor should it cause crippling fear. There is always a way to success and a solution if we are committed to faith and not fear.

> **Baughman:** One of the things that has surprised me in ministry with young professionals and students is that we tend to grow in the summer without really trying. That said, Christmas and the surrounding weeks are our lowest attended because most of our people "go home" around the holidays or are dealing with graduate student exams. I plan to take lessons from Olu's chapter and apply it to our Christmas decline to see what we can do to combat this trend.

I remember dealing with each of these summer realities as we planted our new church. During fear-tempting times like those, I often recall the first day of worship for Impact. It was a cool and slightly rainy day on Sunday, January 7, 2007, when more than three hundred people gathered in a middle school auditorium for our inaugural worship experience. Our team was on cloud nine despite sound system issues, weather challenges, and the hustle and bustle of preparations. Nothing deterred our giving God praise and glory. After that first Sunday, we quickly shifted to the mode of weekly worship, off on a blast, trusting God every step of the way. We had no idea what was next outside of God's hand of favor guiding us. Providentially and without any forethought among our planning crew, having planted in January, Easter was around the corner. We plunged into Easter like a missile homing in on a target. Not missing a step or a beat, we successfully celebrated the Resurrection as a new church. Yet, even with a great new-church launch and an awesome Easter, I knew in the back of my mind that summer was around the corner.

Whatever the reason for summer absence, it always has a cascading negative effect on every important detail related to church growth and stability, in particular: volunteers serving, giving remaining high, and overall attendance staying steady. A significant loss in any one of these key areas can rock the ship of a new church. Even an existing congregation that isn't stable and perhaps lacks reserves or outside support may not be able to survive the summer. This very real concern is one that I believe God cares about, as do those who are contributing wisdom to this wonderful resource book.

But now I say to you . . .

My hope is that you are not totally discouraged after encountering the realities of summer, because hope is also always around the corner. And for people of faith like you and me, this hope isn't only from God. Hope can also come from strategy and planning. So what is the answer? How do you grow in the summer? Before considering strategy, we must shift our mindsets and how we activate our faith. Foundationally, you and your team must be committed to reversing the typical summer decline, the myth that so many congregations have bought into and by which many have allowed themselves to be misguided.

Upon your decision not to accept this seasonal "curse," activate your faith. This step means that we must be willing to believe God for the impossible and to stand firm in faith, no matter what our current attendance or financial realities may be in our local churches. Recently, I was reading Isaiah 7, when Ahaz and Judah were being threatened and God told them not to be afraid or worry. After that admonition God instructed them, "If you do not stand firm in your faith, you will not stand at all" (v. 9). God's word to Ahaz is a reminder to those of us living in the twenty-first century who still believe that we will see the hand and favor of God, that God's greatest blessings are always partnered with great responsibility. As a spiritual leader you have been called to a great work, and it will take faith and courage to see the vision become a reality. Although the journey is difficult you have to believe it is possible and that God will help you achieve the purpose for your life and the local church you are serving.

After deciding not to be guided by a myth and activating your faith, you and your team must establish an agreement. In the early days of launching a new church, 100 percent agreement is virtually impossible, but majority agreement is mandatory. Agreement is essential because it confirms that all involved parties are on the same page, walking the same path. As leaders, we are called to rally the troops around a common cause and trust God for the impossible. This convening means casting vision and making sure that all of your team members (volunteer and staff) are committed to the vision of not declining in the summer in any area. I cannot stress enough the importance of team members being bound to this goal because it is critical to the growth process. If not, one group will be dedicated and burn out trying to make the vision come to fruition, while other groups stand back either to watch the failure take place or to join in the celebration when the vision becomes a reality. In either case, without all members committed, we experience poor teamwork. Having some teams devoted and some not is like a member of your favorite sports team refusing to go to practice, learn the playbook, and play in each game of the season but expecting to join in the celebration of the team's victory at the end of the playoffs. Such behavior is unfair and selfish of a player on a sports team, and it is unfair and selfish as well for a member of a faith community team, especially in a new church setting. When we planted Impact a few years ago, we often repeated, "All hands on deck." This mantra meant that no person or team was more important than another person or team, and we all had to work together to achieve a common goal and vision. One of those common goals was to grow in the summer and not slump under the "curse" of summer decline.

Finally, to grow in the summer requires acts of innovation, an important and often overlooked prerequisite. Simply put, innovation is an ability to see beyond now into the future and creatively build a bridge connecting the two.

Baughman: I'm very grateful for Olu's words about rallying a church to beat the odds. When I first read this chapter, one of our worship gatherings was in significant decline. All indicators suggested that the congregation would dwindle to nothing even though we felt like we were having an incredible experience every week. We went through the practices Olu talks about, committed as a team to defy gravity, developed a plan, and two months later our worship attendance doubled. We now have greater confidence in the viability of this new congregation as well as God's ability to work miracles.

I must admit that I am an innovation junky and spend a great deal of my life reviewing innovation metrics in various organizations, because I believe *all* innovation is applicable to most religious contexts and can serve as inspirational guides. For instance, I recently required that our leadership staff team read a business article about a food company that is seeking to grow through systems adjustments and innovation. You may be wondering, "What does a food industry article have to do with a local church or new church start?" My answer that I shout from the mountaintop: "Everything!" Although food and churches are very different enterprises, any organization's innovation is still innovation and sometimes reading about it in another organization can inspire the same in your organization. Never be afraid to step outside of your ecosystem to see what other people are doing next door.

Of course, many people think they need an exhaustive list of ideas to help them tactically position themselves for growth in the summer. If you're one of those folks, I hope you aren't disappointed with the three ideas I offer. Trust me: these are three effective strategies that will help your new or existing congregation grow in the summer and overcome the summer decline scare. During the warmest months of the year, you should:

- Offer variety.
- Offer the best.
- Offer an incentive.

Now, let's work on the application of each of these summer growth principles. First, always remember to offer variety during the summer months in your local congregation. People in our congregations may choose to remain at home during the summer and may not venture off for long periods of time. Give them a reason to worship with your community.

Baughman: Our summer series tends to focus on issues that no one will talk about but everyone wants to talk about, like death, sex, and how to find meaning while "adulting." These series all seem to draw a lot of interest and drive attendance. On the flip side, I remember other series in churches where I have served. We sold these summer series as "fun" but they were really just "lazy" because, you know, summer. Congregants see through our effort to polish liturgical turds every time.

One year, our team felt summer was a great opportunity to bring the vacation to church and launched two fantastic and innovative series: Theme Park and Vegas. The Theme Park series helped people feel like they were on vacation while attending weekly worship at Impact during the summer. That said, I really fell in love with the Vegas theme series. During this series our worship team sang Vegas-style tunes, dressed up like show superstars, and decorated the stage with Vegas-props. Can you believe that we had oversized playing cards and slot machines on the stage? Remember at the beginning of the chapter I mentioned innovation? In today's world, people want innovation and application that is not limited to the marketplace or their daily lives outside of the church. There are people who like to feel the sacred and the latest innovation in the same context of worship. In most cases, our local churches focus heavily on application and miss innovation opportunities. Variety and innovation inspire worshippers to attend during the summer, because the local church actively works to engage their attention. Congregants deserve to have awesome worship experiences that speak to their need for novelty and desire to have fun during this season. As you know, you will always deal with people who complain that they are tired of ramping up when everyone is ramping down. As a leader you have to be humble enough to hear their concerns but strong enough to move forward in faith and courage to do what is best for your church.

Second, offer the highest quality worship experiences during the summer months supported by volunteers and greeters who meet people with a smile, hug, and kind word as they approach the church parking lot or front door. I will admit that as a pastor I sometimes wonder if I should hold off on a hot, new sermon series until the time of the year with the greatest attendance. Typically such delay means letting up on the gas in the summer. Certainly, our staff and volunteers deserve a break during the summer, but if we are strategic in our planning we can give people a break and still have a fresh crew of volunteers and staff offering their absolute best to worshippers. You can offer a break for your volunteers by planning events and themes well before the summer so volunteers and staff can begin working on ideas, props, programs, and so forth for the upcoming summer themes. In addition to early planning, begin identifying people who will specifically serve during the summer when your consistent volunteers and staff are on break. A key reason excellence in the summer is so important is that regular attendees will eventually figure out if your church's philosophy is to go on hiatus during the summer. If you go on break, they will also disengage and not return until fall.

Let people know that you expect them to come during the summer, and because you expect them to come, you are offering your best. For many of you this strategy won't be easy. What I say to you is that growth is never easy; that is why it is growth. That is why some people subconsciously through their actions—or lack of actions—choose not to grow. Yet, I know you are different and you are willing to do whatever it takes to grow. You have to offer your best. Whether you are reading this chapter close to the summer or just after it, I encourage you to plan now for the upcoming summer experience in your faith community. To accomplish this goal you will have to reengineer parts of your faith community's culture and get those who are already invested in the vision of your church invested again in a new way. This (re)investment means being committed to growing in the summer and not declining.

This undertaking will require that every team (volunteer or staff) pledges to offer their best.

The third key to summer growth is offering an incentive, encouraging worship attendees to be more consistent, and inviting others to join them during the summer. Think about the world we live in and how many for-profit companies offer incentives in the form of rebates or coupons to their customers. These companies realize we live in a world filled with competition. They work constantly to retain existing customers while recruiting new ones. I have often returned to a department store where I was a customer because they sent a coupon in the mail or via email. I have also patronized department stores I normally do not frequent because they reached out to me with a unique reason to enter their space. The same strategy can work for our local churches, especially our new churches. We are living in a time when we are not only competing with other churches for people's attendance, but with Sunday brunch, professional sports, and other activities. Worshippers may not simply come to your church out of a deep sense of religious responsibility, but they will come if they are given the right incentive. Furthermore, they will invite others to attend with them. You may feel this is watering down the mission of the church, but at Impact we know it is simply the result of good evangelism in the twenty-first century.

Not only have we offered a summer incentive but we also have offered incentives when we launched a new initiative. One summer we gave away an electronic tablet each month. Though the cost of purchasing the tablets was significant, it was worth the investment. Walk through this exercise with me. Let's say the tablet investment is $450 times three to cover each month of the summer. The rules for the incentive program specified that a winner would be selected at the end of each month in the summer. Each monthly winner was required to invite and show up with no fewer than ten new people that month to be eligible to win. Although the participant might not know it, the likelihood of winning is high, because typically, not many people participate. (We have discovered that incentive programs are a lot like high school scholarship programs. Many organizations end up with scholarship money in reserve because few students apply.) So, if fifteen people participate in this summer incentive program and only two people each month meet the minimum requirement of ten guests, while the other thirteen people bring five to nine people with them, you have accomplished your incentive goal. With this kind of participation, more new people are added to your local church attendance each month during the summer. You have successfully recruited fifteen people committed to actively evangelizing new people over the summer. You have received a return of the $1,350 spent at the beginning of the summer to purchase the tablets. The new people who attended over the summer surely contributed financially more than $1,350. Truly, if you don't do something unique and creative over the summer, the likelihood is that your congregation will go into decline in both people and money.

I believe God wants your church to grow and not go into decline during the summer. However, you have to decide not to buy into this myth, to commit to activate your faith, to develop an agreement with your team to upend the myth, and to pursue innovation in all things. We cannot expect God to act mightily if we are not committed to helping God in this area by doing our very best.

Here is our recap: Offer variety during the summer so that your attendees know you are actively thinking about them and attempting to capture their attention. Offer your best during the summer because people matter to God and they should matter to you no matter the season of the year. Become known as a church of summer excellence. Finally, offer an incentive during the summer to encourage people to attend regularly and to invite other people to attend. Do all of this and I promise you will have the best summer yet! Let's trust God together for growth and excellence.

Rigid Theology, Big Stages, and Dark Rooms Are Necessary for Worship with Millennials

MICHAEL BAUGHMAN, UNION COFFEE

You have heard it said . . .

Go to most major cities in America and you'll probably find a church teeming with twenty-somethings. It's large. They've got screens bigger than your rented church meeting space. All of their ministries are named with power words like *impact, elevate,* or *soar.* Sometimes they use compound words that start with "cross," like *crosswalk, crosstrain, crossover, crossword,* or simply *crossings* (but probably not *crossdress*). When they crank up the bass on the sound system, it registers somewhere on the Richter scale. You might even own a CD from their house band—not because you like the theology, but because their music is so dang catchy. Maybe it's their Christmas album. Their lighting specialist does contract work for Beyoncé, and you sometimes stop at their coffee bar on the way to your church because their lattes are so good. You can't stand their theology but can't ignore their success at attracting young people.

Michael Baughman is the Community Curator and founding pastor for Union Coffee in Dallas, Texas. ◆ uniondallas.org

> **Herships:** Yes! This drives me nuts! It feels like they're treating the Church as a "product." Sadly, we (the Church) are the ones that have trained church-goers to think of church as a product. I love that Mike is naming it here!

It makes sense we think we need to be like them. They do a lot of things right that more churches should attend to—emphasize visual aesthetics for an image-driven culture, put out top-notch communications coupled with clear plans for discipleship and follow through. We have a lot to learn from them. Undoubtedly, some young people will only attend worship that is as good as the Beyoncé, Katy Perry, Ed Sheeran, or Taylor Swift extravaganza they experienced last month. We often believe that we need the same stuff professional performers use—the same black-and-white theology, the same production values, the same music experience—and we just can't compete with their finances or bring ourselves to proclaim neo-Calvinist theology without throwing up in our mouths a little. So we give up or we spend a bunch of time trying to mimic the high production values that we just can't recreate on a minimal budget.

They're connecting with a particular demographic and they do it well. I'm glad for their success. My ministry is with young people—but they're a very different group from the ones attending the local megachurch.

But I say to you . . .

For every five hundred young professionals who attend worship at the area megachurch, I am convinced that there are thousands who walk in their doors, get involved, and then leave as they find out it is not the place for them. There are thousands more who never set foot in the doors of a church that has previously burned or bored them. The harvest is huge and the workers are few. The church devotes precious few resources to connecting with rising generations, let alone learning from them and allowing them to lead worship that is authentic to their unique style of learning. Here's the great irony: we have shaped Millennials into becoming the generation that they are by raising them very differently from the way their parents were raised. Still, most of our ministries try to change them back into something more like their parents.

Before I go into the lessons I've learned about worshipping with Millennials, it is worth offering a caveat: they aren't all the same (*gasp*). Any blog post, book, chapter, or tweet that offers you *what Millennials* really *want* will probably just reveal what the author wants Millennials to really want—my own chapter included.

> **Herships:** This is so true! I feel myself start to rage when any expert starts going on and on about what "fill-in-the-blank people group needs." There seems to be such fear around the church dying that everyone is looking for the magic bullet. It simply doesn't exist. I love doing AfterHours. . . . I also know it isn't a fit for everybody. We are not everyone's beverage of choice . . . and that's OK.

The economic, social, and educational realities that have shaped this generation have never before been seen on the face of the earth. These realities are so fresh, it is difficult to predict much about the brave new world that the largest generation on the planet has to offer. My experiences with church outsiders may be different from yours, but in conversation we may find a better way to be in ministry with this incredible generation.

Questionable Faith

For a generation raised on Google, questions are currency. Armed with a browser and a good question, a person can be entertained, inspired, and educated for hours as she links from one idea to a video of cats to a show on Netflix that she needs to binge watch. This generation has been educated with a critical pedagogy that dissects the world with interrogative exploration, leaving lectures and lists behind. They are creatures of mass deconstruction.

When a team at Union (the new church start I lead) decided to curate a worship gathering called Studio for Dallas artists and corporate young professionals, we decided to craft a creed to clarify what it is that would bring our community together. We found that questions can define us as much as answers. It's distinctly Wesleyan and faithful to the Christian tradition. Our community shares in this creed at the beginning of worship each week.

> *What if God never stopped creating?*
> *What if God crafts mosaics from the broken pieces of yesterday, clears canvases for a fresh start, and offers hope to a world in need?*
>
> *What if certainty was the opposite of faith?*
> *What if faith is a choice that gives life because of our questions, not in spite of them?*
>
> *What if Jesus came to give us more than forgiveness, more than healing, more than wisdom?*
> *What if Jesus gives us a story that shapes our story so that we might shape the world?*
>
> *What if we knew our purpose and had a place, regardless of where we're from, what we believe, or whom we love?*
> *What if that place is here?*
>
> *What if we are already creators, collaborators, and friends with God?*
> *What if we're a part of God's story for Dallas?*
>
> *What if we live like these things are true?*

As we wrote our creed, we realized the value of question marks. Most creeds are full of periods. Periods make a statement. Periods draw a line that either includes me or does not. Question marks, however, have the opportunity to invite.

> **Ruffle:** In the congregation that I am a part of, we also find ourselves asking a lot of questions about the way we worship and encounter our neighbors in mission. We haven't yet formulated a creed with "what if" questions (though we might take a stab at that), but we question many of the assumptions of our greed infested, gun-loving generation.

Question marks—especially when prefaced with an aspirational phrase like "what if"—make room for those who do not find themselves ready to sign on the dotted line. They draw the listener in and offer a possibility of discipleship or faith even if they do not yet believe. Sometimes we assume that question marks, because they are interrogative, strip the preceding words of weight or definition. We find that our questions say as much about us as any definitive statement. You can probably discern a lot about our community, who we attract, and what we stand for based on the questions that we ask. In my experience, questions can reveal a lot about the individuals who ask them as well.

Many churches encourage their congregants to ask questions. While this is all well and good, sometimes church leaders are comfortable asking questions as long as the people come to the "right" conclusions. This leads to tension between the church and questioner, which confuses the one who is asking the question, because he believed the church leader when she said that his is a church that welcomes questions.

Questions cannot be controlled. Questions are unpredictable. Questions find a way to break out of the boxes of polity, practice, and doctrine we put in place to make everything a little more manageable.

The very things that make us nervous about questions are what give them power. Questions are holy, and if Jacob taught me anything it's that wrestling with God leads to a blessed identity— even if you walk away with a limp. The more we give young people the opportunity to explore questions in worship as well as study, the better. Our sermons at Union are always conversational. It's common for someone to stick their hand up in worship and say, "Mike, I think what you're saying is bullshit, and this is why. . . ." Then we enter into conversation. I can't tell you the number of sermons that went into a totally different direction from what our team had prepared. While that may feel chaotic to some, it feels like the Holy Spirit to me.

I believe that encouraging questions in sermons is possible in both large and small settings, though more intimate settings are a more natural fit for such interactions. Through the creative use of technology and a brave willingness to be put on the spot, questions can become a celebrated and integral part of worship. One of my favorite sermons to do is completely "questionable." I prepare nothing. Every congregant is given a note card (in more tech savvy places, worshipers can simply text) and asked to write a question about faith, the church, life, or whatever matters to them. Then, their questions are collected, and a moderator asks me questions from the stack. I have three minutes to answer each question. Half the time, I put the question to the congregation to see what comes out of the body. On a speedy night, I make it through ten questions selected from a much bigger stack. That leftover stack shapes the next several months of preaching and gives me insight into my congregation. *That leftover stack is gold.*

There are many ways to incorporate questions into worship. Congregants can ask or tweet on the spot. Small groups can be designed to carry forward the conversation that begins in worship on Sunday. Testimony and sermons can be shared through an interview format. The possibilities are only limited by our creativity and willingness to risk. Asking questions is not enough, however. Our first worshipping community at Union excelled at deconstructing Christianity for our first six months of gatherings. People who had been burned by the church flocked to it at first. After this initial burst, we watched attendance become steadily less regular and then it started to really decline. We realized that we had spent so much time deconstructing but never put theology, beliefs, or biblical interpretation back together in a new, more robust, and faithful way. Even in a culture dominated by snark, no one wants to hang out in a community that is always complaining.

Questions became the entry point for new ideas. Through our work to reconstruct practices of faith that were more meaningful than what we had traditionally known, we found new ways to understand discipleship. We saw God at work, making all things new. Our best ideas about God, faith, discipleship, and life have come out through this process. The reconstructive work of one sermon series leads to an idea for a new one. We discover new ways to understand the scriptures. In so doing, the Holy Spirit is resurrecting the biblical story in the lives of those who thought it to be dead and meaningless.

> **Herships:** I love this whole section on questions. We often admit we don't have it figured out at AfterHours. The power doesn't come from answers, it comes from the freedom to ask the question! And truly, is there anyone who actually BELIEVES he or she has it figured out when it comes to God? It reminds me of the quote from St. Augustine, "We are talking about God. . . . If you do understand, then it is not God."

Work of the People Planning

No sermons or services at Union are planned solo. At thirty-seven, with my own children spanning from ages six to fourteen, I'm at least two life-stages removed from the primary constituency of our congregation. The average age of those who worship with me is twenty-four and a half. If I planned our worship gatherings on my own, most young professionals would likely find them to be old and out of touch. I am only able to be in effective ministry with people so young because they lead in planning worship and in executing most of the worship gathering. My job is to observe and point—to what God is doing, to what is broken in our neighborhood, to what Jesus says, and to what is affecting the lives of the people in my care. Their job is to figure out what we, as a community, should do about it, how it impacts the way we worship God, and how our worship should reflect that impact. Each week my worship design teams of young professionals and college students dedicate two hours of their lives to sitting with me and planning worship. We evaluate last week, sketch out the sermons for the coming weeks, and design worship elements around the core message. I usually brain-dump ideas about where the sermon might go. The team identifies what will likely connect with our congregation, educates me on what I don't know/understand/experience about their lives, and together we craft a flow for each sermon.

> **Ruffle:** I find convergence among Union and generationally-distant communities of faith. The congregation that I attend also has a team that plans worship together. Worship, then, is the work of the people. It sounds like a similar setup, our people just happen to be older.

Planning a sermon by committee can be a disaster to some, but it's when I find my best creativity is unlocked. It also removes much of the pressure on the preacher. When we debrief a worship gathering gone wrong, fingers of blame aren't pointed at me. Everyone in the room uses "we" language to describe where we went wrong in planning. Likewise, when a worship gathering is amazing, we celebrate and own the victory together. Planning as a team makes us more than relevant. It commits us to one another and this crazy calling to lead worship.

Successful group planning requires honesty and trust, which lead to better results. I have to know that the people in that room have my back no matter what and they have to know that I have theirs. This allows us to be comfortable enough with each other to share ideas that may be absurd, brilliant, or sometimes offensive. This is the kind of space necessary for true creativity. Our worship planning teams are super transparent about things that don't work as well as celebratory about things that do. Through this process, those who felt they had little to contribute find their voice. Atheists who serve on our worship design team learn that they can positively shape the development of a community, and I am constantly excited by new ideas and perspectives on the elements that shape a worshipping community.

As a result of this process, we have had prayers of confession with refrains from Kanye. Most of our hymns come from the radio but nonetheless speak to the soul of our congregation. Our closing song every week *is* a traditional hymn—a choice we made because a team member pointed out that the songs of the homeland matter to a refugee, whether they are estranged from a different country or church they grew up in. YouTube clips, infographics, newly invented two by twos, and *Pecha Kucha*–style sermons make appearances in our worship. We worship "in the round" to see each other's faces and increase participation in congregational singing. Announcements are kept short by requiring people to tweet their announcement instead of standing up and talking forever. All of these ideas make our worship unique and meaningful to the demographic we serve. All of these ideas flow out of the community of trust that plans our worship gatherings from week to week.

Early in the development of our first worshipping community, we committed ourselves to celebrating Communion in worship each week and began experimenting with Communion liturgies that would be meaningful for people who have left or never attended church. Ideas from the team were tried and evaluated. Almost none of these worked. At one point, a member of the team said to me, "I could tell you were really excited about Communion, but it was in the way that an eleven-year-old gets really excited about *Pokemon*. It's like, I can tell you are *really* into this, but I have no idea why." Did I mention that we're really honest with our feedback?

Herships: Having grown up Catholic, Communion, this holy mystery, carries a lot of meaning for me. We have gone from never doing it at AfterHours to always doing it, to now doing it once a month. (Part of this is honestly is due to the logistics of gathering our community in four different venues a month.) I also had to be honest in asking the question, "Are we doing this because it's best for the community or just because Jerry wants it?" Sometimes I don't like the answer, but I'm getting better.

After several months, I tried a simple storytelling approach. I told stories from the Old and New Testaments that reflected the night's message. I talked about the Last Supper and used the words of institution. I prayed about how God could change us through this meal and invited everyone to join in the meal. I acknowledged that some people may not be want to participate in Communion and told the room, that's OK. While people were receiving, I noticed a particular member of our design team stand up. She hadn't taken Communion at any point in our three months of worship. After taking

Communion, she came up to me, wrapped her arms around my neck, and thanked me. She had grown up in the Methodist church and was an active part of leading the Wesley foundation at her college. When her annual conference pulled all funding for campus ministry, she left the church with her middle finger in the air. For the first time in years she heard Communion presented in a way that made sense to her again. It was just casual enough, just invitational enough, and just holy enough for her to give Communion and the church another shot. We've followed that story format every week since.

> **Herships:** I am always amazed at the power of narrative theology (storytelling). I think it is such an underused tool in our toolbox (which is ironic, considering how often Jesus taught with story).

Work of the People in Worship

After the sermon planning sessions, I spend whatever time I can over the next couple days to put flesh on the sermonic skeleton crafted by the team. At the point when I wrap up my preparations, I know that the Holy Spirit's work is not done.

Well-crafted worship involves more than just the people who meet in our coffee shop conference room to plan the weekly gatherings. We are always looking for ways to include the community in directing the message through their participation in worship. Worship gatherings at Union put a high premium on conversation throughout the service. Sometimes all of our hard work and sermon planning results in a sermon that ends with, *So, what the hell does this all mean for us?* and we, in the planning room, have no idea how to answer that question. When we are brave enough to open that unanswered question to the worshipping assembly, the Holy Spirit works in the people, and we find ourselves in the place God needs us to be.

The work of the people extends beyond helping to craft and responding to the sermon. On Sunday nights, we invite local Dallas artists to share their work—songs, monologues, visual art pieces, and more have been offered on our small stage during worship. Almost none of their contributions are overtly religious. I sit and scribble notes while they perform. Later, I incorporate their words and work into the sermon and communion liturgy.

> **Ruffle:** This is an outstanding practice for churches in cities with artistic talent. Located just blocks away from Nashville's "Music Row," the church I attend also draws from the artistic talent of our neighborhood. Some of the artists here include award-winning singer/songwriters. We also have poets and prophets who make waves with their pens and presence at rallies for justice. And, we, too, have made a commitment to celebrate Communion each week. One of the affirmations we make forms the first line of our liturgy: "Everyone has a place at this table." All means all. Maybe these principles transcend the generations.

The church has done a terrible job with the arts community over the past several decades. Inviting artists who have never worshipped with us before, offering them a venue to share their gifts, and then lifting those contributions up as holy, has been one of the best things we've done to restore the church's credibility with a disconnected demographic. As a result, we've cultivated a community of grace, love, and brave vulnerability that extends beyond the artists themselves.

A Dallas musical theater star, Morgan Mabry, stepped onto our Sunday night stage to perform in worship. She began singing "Gravity" by Sara Bareilles—a song about trying to escape the pull of a hurtful relationship. What most people in the room didn't know is that the next morning she would head down to a Dallas courthouse and finalize her divorce. Morgan was singing auto-biographically. After a verse and the chorus, she broke down in tears. She couldn't sing. Our accompanist vamped for a bit while she cried on stage. A woman in the congregation stood up and asked, "Do you need us to sing it for you, baby?" She and two other incredible disciples of Jesus Christ stood to sing the next verse and chorus for Morgan while she wept silently.

Morgan stepped back up to the microphone. She sang the chorus again and the other women sat down. Morgan belted the bridge and finished the song with resolve, triumph, and the kind of tenacious beauty that only comes from those who know grace.

The most powerful moments that night were not scripted but reminded everyone in the room that we are a community who sings one another's songs when we can't do so ourselves. By continually celebrating brave vulnerability and nurturing a participatory spirit, our worshipping communities have progressively claimed worship as theirs. Moments like these—though not always so dramatic—happen on a regular basis. I am blessed to be able to sit back and watch God work through these incredible people that I am called to serve.

> **Herships:** I love that Marcus Borg referred to these moments as "Thin Places," those spots where the holy seems so close you can almost touch it.

This participatory and innovative spirit springs from worship into other aspects of our community life. As our Tuesday night worship communities have matured over the past two years, they've progressively claimed leadership of our community in more than just worship. With little or no assistance on my part, they started planning social events, then small groups, then entire nonprofit spinoff organizations. Recently, our *Kuneo* worship gathering has begun making the connection between worship and our work in the world more overt.

After someone from the congregation tells a story about why they love Union and passes the basket to ask for donations, I stand in front of the congregation and tell them about community needs: a nonprofit agency that needs volunteers, members of our community who need pastoral care, outreach opportunities to members who haven't been present at Union for a while, events at Union that need people to execute. I ask for volunteers on the spot. Hands go up, and I jot down their information and follow up with them later in the week to get them what they need in order to do the work of the church. Sometimes I'll point out upcoming events and then acknowledge that all of us have an inner eighth grader who won't show up at something unless we know people we like will be there. I ask who is willing to be brave and say that they will be there no matter what. Hands go up and more people end up attending because they know friends will be there.

> **Herships:** I don't know if I could ever get the AfterHours people to say they will be there "no matter what." Our average member's age is thirty-five. They just won't make that kind of commitment to "the establishment" even if that is me! I do love the fact that our folks get together a number of times in the week between Mondays. They have truly become community and always seem to open the circle wider. Eighth grade or not, we wanna go where our friends are.

The offering for us is about more than dollars and cents and online donations. It has become our opportunity to set expectations for our community to serve, sacrifice, innovate, care, tell stories, show up, and make our neighborhood a better place. It signals to visitors that these are people who act on their faith. The practices of a church in worship shape the community after the last "amen" is offered. Worship gatherings that give ownership to the people produce apostles who own the work of the church.

Kissing God

Good worship allows for and acknowledges the needs of the people who you hope will connect with God. As an acknowledgment of this, Union's Tuesday night worship gathering is called *Kuneo*. It comes from the Greek word for worship, *proskuneo*. Literally it means "toward kissing." We believe that good worship is a lot like good kissing. People anticipate a good kiss. It leaves someone feeling different. We get to know someone in a new way when we kiss him or her. Sometimes it's messy or awkward, and that's okay too. Most important, good kissing happens when both parties are concerned with the desires, comforts, experiences, needs, and emotions of one another. I believe that the megachurches are full of young people who are legitimately experiencing a divine presence that shapes their lives. The worship we see in megachurches with young people reflects the needs of mainstream evangelical students. Church refugees, outsiders, and the religiously nonaffiliated have different needs. The signature of their kiss is different. At Union, we strive to match the contour of their lips.

The most innovative elements of our worship gatherings are difficult to execute on a big stage in a dark room with all the chairs pointed in one direction. We've been blessed enough to tap into a growing young community of church refugees who are longing for a spiritual home unlike the one they left. These are the high-hanging fruit that are difficult to touch. These are the outsiders for whom we must become more "vile," as Wesley would call them, in order to offer them hope of the gospel. These are the renegades, rebels, and trailblazers who will mature the church for a younger generation.

Herships: Rebels and trailblazers—love that. At AfterHours they will often refer to each other as Rogue Disciples.

Once upon a time, the Methodist movement took off because a handful of college students and young professionals decided to live holier lives. Everything the United Methodist Church is—every congregation and university, every UMCOR (United Methodist Committee on Relief) effort and publication—comes as a result of their efforts. If today we empower the young to prophesy and lead, maybe God will revive us again with the power of God's kiss.

Churches Go into Prisons, They Aren't in Prisons

DIANE HARRISON, GRACE PLACE UNITED METHODIST CHURCH

You have heard it said . . .

I know I have heard it said that we should *visit* those who are in prison but to actually have a church inside the prison? Inviting convicted criminals to be a part of the church seems odd. After hearing God's call to start a church in prison, I had to accept that Jesus, a convicted criminal, knew what he was talking about when he gave my life direction. A church in a prison is an upside down, radical, countercultural idea that sounds just like the kingdom of God.

I had just completed my third Kairos, four-day retreat weekend at the Mark Luttrell Correctional Center for Women, a state prison in Memphis, Tennessee. The course presented Christianity to inmates through a series of talks. Each of those three weekends I had heard one of the team members give a talk to

---

Diane Harrison is the founding pastor for Grace Place United Methodist Church inside the Mark Luttrell Correctional Center in Memphis, Tennessee. ◆ graceplacemethodist.com

the women about the church and how important it was for each of them to become a part of a worshipping community once the weekend was over. But there wasn't a church in the prison! There were lots of churches that came in and held worship services, but that's not a church. Many groups came in and held Bible studies and seminars to indoctrinate people in the faith, but that wasn't a church either.

> **Ross:** The fleeting-encounter model seems to be the status quo for the church's ministry with all marginalized populations. To the marginalized, the church says, "We'll give you soup, school supplies, and maybe a sermon, but we are not ready to be in a Sunday school class with you."

At the end of each weekend my heart broke as I said goodbye to these women we had come to love and call sisters. What would happen to them when we left? How could they make it in the dark world called prison that they would wake up to the next day? The more I prayed and thought about it, the clearer I heard and understood what the Lord was asking me to do—plant a church in the prison. They needed a church. They needed to be a church. They needed a community of faith made up of residents of the prison who were, as it says in the mission statement they subsequently wrote for their church, "Seeking, seeing, and serving God inside and outside the prison walls."

But I say to you . . .

Now I know what you're thinking. Don't they have a chaplain? Yes, our prison has a chaplain, but the chaplain is not the "pastor" for the women. Much of the chaplain's time is spent scheduling activities, training, certifying and recertifying volunteers, as well as other administrative tasks. The chapel is really a sacred space set aside for use by all the residents of the prison and the chaplain is there for all the women regardless of their faith tradition. According to the rules of many prisons, the chaplain is to avoid "proselytizing" in order to serve everyone. In fact, many prisons have begun calling the chaplain "director of religious services."

So yes, they needed a church: a twenty-four-hours-a-day faith community made up of incarcerated women with an outside pastor supported by the church on the outside. In the beginning my denominational "powers that be" couldn't quite grasp the concept, so they said we couldn't be a new church plant. Because only inmates would join, a church in a prison would be "restricting the membership." But they did agree to allow us to start an "extension ministry" that would be "tethered" to an existing "free world" congregation. We also needed to understand that we would be 100 percent responsible for our financial support, including all pastoral support. We accepted these terms and began the difficult challenge of planting a church under the guise of being a prison ministry.

A new church start in a prison is very different from a traditional prison ministry, where the inmates are the recipients of the efforts of the free-world volunteers. A prison congregation sees inmates as not only *recipients* of God's love and grace but *agents* of God's love and grace. This would be *their* church. They would provide the lay leadership and do the work of the church. Jesus calls us to make disciples, and disciples serve.

> **Ross:** I am continually amazed by the survival skills of marginalized people. To see this ingenuity channeled to make disciples enables the church to do things that nonmarginalized pastors and congregants could never even imagine.

So this church would be a church engaged in mission and out-reach. How to begin? We had many obstacles to overcome.

> We had a bishop who didn't believe you could even have a
> church in a prison.
> We had no money.
> We didn't know what the prison would allow us to do.
> We didn't know what a church in a prison would look like.
> We didn't know how the residents would respond. Did they
> even feel the need for a church?

Ross: I began Christ's Foundry erroneously asking people what they needed. I guess I should not have been surprised that none of the Spanish-speaking immigrants in our community said, "What we really need is a United Methodist Church." I should have started by asking, "I have felt called to start a church in this community. Will you help me?"

Could we overcome the traditional view of what it meant to be engaged in ministry *to* prisoners and instead be in ministry *with* prisoners?

At that point we didn't really even have a "we." But soon we did. A small group of supporters on the outside and a district super-intendent were bold enough to ask others to help us. We needed money and we needed it quick. I prayed and asked the Lord where to get it, and the Lord told me who to ask. I asked my brother and sister-in-law if they would be willing to give us the money to cover our budget for the first year. I wrote them a letter, because I didn't have enough nerve to call them. I drove to the post office and sat at the drive-up mailbox, held the letter in my hand, and prayed for the Lord to help them receive it in the way I intended. In two weeks I had a check. I learned we have to be bold. Taking risks is hard for me, a shy person, but I learned God uses all kinds of people in ways we could never imagine.

We began as Jesus began: with a small group. A small group of supporters inside signed up to do Disciple Bible Study. Twelve women incarcerated at the prison signed up to be a part of this thirty-four session, two-and-a-half-hours-a-week study. It is a Bible study for transformation, not information. I called them the Twelve Apostles of Grace Place. Oh yes, we had a name, "Grace Place," because everyone needs a place of grace. Soon after our Disciple Bible Study began we also started a book club. This was not a Christian book club but a club for people who wanted to read books and have discussions with others about what they had read.

> **Garber:** This is why the word *Christian*, when used as an adjective, can be so limiting. Kudos to Diane for not allowing the label to limit outreach or vision.

It was designed as a way to reach women who did not choose, for a variety of reasons, to participate in any "religious" activities at the prison. It began in October 2007 and is still going strong. That October we also had our first worship service. We met at noon on Saturday, a terrible time to try to have worship, as Saturday was a visitation day, but it was the only time they had available in the schedule. So noon it was.

During the early months of planting our congregation, someone suggested I obtain a publication put out by The General Board of Discipleship of my denomination (United Methodist) called "Prison Ministry Toolbox." I ordered it and when it came I eagerly searched through the pages of ideas for churches wanting to be engaged in prison ministry. Much to my surprise I turned a page and it said, "You might even want to start a church in a prison." If you did, it suggested you contact Prison Congregations of America, an organization whose mission is to help mainline denominations plant churches in prisons. It was started by Pastor Ed Nesselhuf,

of the Evangelical Lutheran Church in America, who had pastored a prison congregation himself. I immediately e-mailed
Nesselhuf, and before long he came to Memphis to see what we
were doing and how he could help. One of the best things he told
me was there was another prison congregation in The United
Methodist Church in a prison at the Mitchellville Correctional
Center for Women in Mitchellville, Iowa. It was called Women
at the Well United Methodist Church. What wonderful news this
was. I have worshipped with Women at the Well UMC, and both
their founding and current pastors have worshipped with Grace
Place. One of the wonderful things about a church in the prison is
how ecumenical it is. We have women who don't want to become
Methodist but do want to be a part of a faith community in which
they can live out their call to discipleship. I have learned so much
from brothers and sisters in other denominations who are also
engaged in leading a prison congregation. How beautiful is the
body of Christ.

During the first year of Grace Place we added an exercise class
and a study group and, most important, we formed our inside
church council made up of nine residents of the prison and the
pastor. We also have an outside council made up of volunteers and
supporters who take care of fiduciary and personnel matters, lead
small groups, and help fund raise and support our congregation in
a million different ways.

The real work of our church is done by the women inside. By
being open to new ways of doing things and using creative thinking
to get around, over, and under obstacles, we have grown a congregation that does a remarkable amount of mission outreach inside
and outside the prison. When we wanted to do something that
didn't seem possible within the confines of the prison, we chan-
neled the creative ingenuity that abounds at a prison into positive
outcomes. We don't work alone and often partner with the outside.
For example, outside folks donate yarn. Inside folks use their skills

to transform that yarn into hats and scarves that we distribute to organizations in our community that serve marginalized people. We have given over five hundred sets of handmade hats and scarves to the outside population in Memphis. When I drive through Memphis in the winter, I frequently see men and women walking down the street and proudly say, "There go some of our hats and scarves." It is a beautiful circle of cooperation that allows women in prison to be in ministry to needy and homeless people.

Engaging the inside population in ministry work is both empowering and healing, because the women know they are making a difference in the outside world as well as the inside prison population. We sell items made by our women such as crocheted bears and bookmarks, angels and reindeer, original artwork, devotionals and cookbooks written by our members.

> **Ross:** I can only imagine how this transforms the self-perception of these women.

As a result, our women have raised and donated over $4,500 to mission outreach over three years. They've used this money to benefit Memphis in ways like purchasing a picnic table to be used in the shady backyard of a hospitality house for homeless people. They have supplied Easter outfits and backpacks full of school supplies for children in need. They purchased a Personal Energy Transporter, a self-powered cart for disabled people, which was given to a woman in the Dominican Republic. They provided rice and beans for a family in Costa Rica for a year. They have also sent money to support No More Malaria and assisted earthquake victims in Nepal. My church members are committed to making the world a better place—regardless of prison boundaries.

The church where my office is located in Memphis serves a lunch every Monday to anyone in the community who would like to come. It is in a very economically depressed area. There are always hungry people there. Many different churches volunteer to provide the lunches. The pastor of the church came to me at the end of the year and said, "One of the churches that has been doing six lunches a year has just told me they will only be able to do three next year. Do you think your ladies would be willing to pick up the other three?" I told him of course they wouldn't be able to come and serve it but that they might be willing to pay for the food. He said we could do a meal for about $250. I took it to the inside church council, and they agreed to make the ongoing commitment of $750 a year. Now a ministry in the outside world counts on us. Women in prison feeding the hungry in the free world! Yes, I'd say that is a radical, upside down, countercultural idea.

By being a church rather than a chaplaincy, we are better able to care for the needs of inmates. Our very faithful member's mother was in hospice care. We knew the time of her death was very close, and word came that her mother had died at a time when I didn't happen to be in the prison. My volunteers and I are only allowed to be there during times when we have scheduled activities. The chaplain was not there that day either. The inmates got word to one of our outside volunteers, who was distressed that none of us could be there for the inmate whose mother had died. I told her not to worry. She'll be okay because the church is there! They will take care of her, love her, pray with her, and be the presence of Christ with her, and indeed they were. We need a church in the prison for the same reasons we all need the church: to be there in times of need.

One of the inside ministries our church is engaged in is sending birthday cards to every woman in the prison on her birthday. The inside council members and I all sign the cards and send them out. To those of us in the free world, a birthday card might not seem like a big thing. One day I was walking down the hall at the prison and a woman who is not a part of Grace Place saw me and said, "Hi Pastor Diane, thanks for the birthday card." "Oh, you're welcome," I said. She started down the hall and then stopped and turned to me and said, "You know, if I hadn't gotten that birthday card, I would have forgotten that it was my birthday." I will never forget that day and how much it made me realize the significance of little things. To be honest, I used to dread the day we pass the cards around and have to sign our names over and over, but now I know it is a sacred act, reminding those who think they have been forgotten that they are loved, they are important, and that the day they were born was a great day. Sending a card is such a simple thing.

> **Ross:** This is a simple but true act of sharing the good news that each and every person is important to God. This birthday card ministry inspires me to think about what Christ's Foundry can do to recognize those who so often go unrecognized.

So many people in prison have no family, or the family they do have has given up on them. One of our members told me once, "I still write my family even though they don't write me. I just want them to know that I am still alive."

All of our small groups are led by free world volunteers. We have clergy and laypeople who come each week to facilitate these groups.

> **Garber:** I'm curious if there is a plan to start small groups led by church members "on the inside." I wonder if there's a potential advantage of groups led by persons on the "inside" as well as the "outside."

They come from different churches and denominations and reflect the diversity of our church. They help us connect the free world to the hidden world of the prison. They are, in a sense, human icons who provide a window through which the inside and the outside world can see each other in a new way. Those on the inside are now equal partners with outside disciples engaged in the life and work of the church. I learned from my very wise brother that in any organization, people are your greatest asset. I have never seen this more clearly than when I observe this partnership.

We finally did become an official chartered United Methodist Church. I was given fifteen minutes to present the Grace Place story to the bishop and the cabinet. That day they voted unanimously to make us a mission congregation. We still are responsible for raising 100 percent of our funding, but it meant so much to our church to be able to call ourselves Grace Place United Methodist Church. Several months later our new bishop came and held a service of consecration for our church, and we received our first thirteen charter members. It was a day I will never forget. A woman who would barely say her name when she first came to our church stood and read scripture before the bishop preached. She was a new creature in Christ. One of the most important things I have learned is that when God calls, we must persevere, even when the church says no. Finally, after five long years, we were acknowledged as a church.

I am so proud of our congregation. We are ethnically diverse. We are not an African American church or a white church or a Latino church or Asian church. We are all of those. We work together. Our Spanish-speaking group is growing.

Baughman: Reading Diane's chapter, I'm inspired by how her congregation successfully executes so many of the things we say the Methodist church should be about—empowered and equipped lay leadership, ministry *with* the marginalized, ethnic diversity. I hope that her story will inspire others to do and be likewise.

We include the lectionary readings in every service, and one is always read in Spanish. Our liturgist is an African American woman who has been in prison since 2006 for a first-degree murder conviction in the perpetration of aggravated child abuse. Yes, that is hard to hear. But at Grace Place we come to the table every week and we love the words, "Christ died for us while we were yet sinners. That proves God's love for us. In the name of Jesus Christ you are forgiven." She does a magnificent job and serves on our inside council. She believes that she has a calling, and I believe she has a calling. So I ask myself, "Lord, is it possible that you are calling a woman in prison to preach?" Maybe she could be a pastor in the prison. Did Jesus not say, "For mortals it is impossible, but for God all things are possible" (Matt. 19:26, NRSV)?

Our church is alive, vibrant, and fully engaged. We do not let the fact that we are in a prison and have many restrictions hinder us. Our church is liturgical. We celebrate and observe the church year. We begin with Advent. Our church has a chrismon tree, with chrismons made by our members, and an advent wreath, though our candles are battery powered. Our choir prepares special music just as any other church, and we always have a Christmas Eve Communion service. We have an Ash Wednesday service, and during Holy Week we always have a seder meal and stations of the cross in both English and Spanish. We have Easter sunrise services. We use the same liturgies and pass the same peace. We are connected through these acts with all other Christians who claim them as expressions of their faith. Our members hold up the light in the dark recesses of the prison where free world volunteers are not allowed to go. We are the church.

Baughman: There is such a Wesleyan spirit about Diane's work. We forget far too often that the early Methodists put a high premium on visiting prisoners. Grace Place has lived into and amplified the early Methodists by building authentic church community within the walls of the prison system.

I have learned a lot on this journey. When I heard the call to plant this church, the Lord coaxed me like someone learning to dive. "Jump, Diane! Jump into this new adventure I have for you! I will catch you." The first time I heard that call, I was afraid. It was two years before I was ready to make that leap. I discovered faith doesn't come with a timeline. It comes with a promise: "I will be with you." I learned that even the craziest, most far-fetched idea might be just what the Lord has in mind, like when he called little David to take on a giant or asked a little boy to give up his basket of bread and fish to feed a multitude or called Noah to build an ark. All answering God's call requires is faith and creativity. If we have the faith, God will supply us with the creativity. After all, God is the original creator. The very first thing revealed to us about God in scripture is that God created. God created heaven and earth and you and me. And because we are not only God's creation, but created in God's image, we too have the ability to create. God is always creating, always making something new, sometimes out of something old. I have learned that to plant a new church is to partner with God in the act of creating. Every time our church, Grace Place, is presented with a challenge, we get creative and figure out a way to meet that challenge. Our church powerfully demonstrates the truth of God's forgiveness, redemption, and restoration. Women inside a prison can be the church, not objects of the church's pity or compassion, not "children of a lesser god," but equal partners in the life and work of the church. Thanks be to God.

Garber: Amen! This story is inspiring, encouraging, and empowering!

Planting Churches Requires Clergy

ELAINE HEATH, MISSIONAL WISDOM FOUNDATION

You have heard it said, but I say to you . . .

Perhaps the biggest myth about church planting today in the United Methodist Church is that church planting is for professionals. That idea, along with all other fallacies that limit "real" ministry to clergy, has no basis in scripture or the original Methodist vision. Rather these are notions that emerge from and help to perpetuate established institutional structures within the denomination including guaranteed appointments for clergy and the expectation that persons seeking ordination must plan to earn their living from the church. These systems evolved in the first half of the twentieth century but are no longer sustainable. That observation may sound dire, but it is the way things are.

Elaine Heath is the dean of Duke Divinity School in Durham, North Carolina. She is the cofounder of the Missional Wisdom Foundation, which has planted New Day Communities across Dallas and Fort Worth, Texas. ◆ missionalwisdom.com

> **Baughman:** I'm five sentences into Elaine's chapter and I'm already uncomfortable. I'm not sure if it's because I disagree with her on merit or if I just want to believe that my work in the ordination process matters and that I want to protect my own value. Either way, I'm interested in what she has to say!

One of the signposts of this shift is the increase in numbers of churches that can only afford a part-time, bivocational pastor.[1] In the past decade in the Western Pennsylvania Conference, for example, the number of part-time local pastors has doubled. In Oklahoma over 250 congregations have total budgets under $80,000, so a full-time clergy is out of the question.[2] Many people view this as a negative development that is helping to bring about the demise of the United Methodist Church. However, something wonderful in the realm of church planting is emerging from the detritus of our failing systems. And that exciting turn of events—the development of laypeople to use their God-given gifts for ministry in church planting—is what I want to focus on in this chapter. To get there, let's begin with some foundations in scripture and our own Methodist tradition. What does the Bible say about church planters? How did Methodism start and then thrive early on?

Alan Hirsch, a leading voice in the ecumenical missional church planting movement, describes historical and contemporary church planting movements that the church needs to learn from, including early Methodism. As Hirsch notes, the reason Methodism grew so much in its first century was that it was primarily a lay movement in which laypersons had a high degree of involvement in leading disciple-making ministry.[3]

Hirsch explains that three of the five-fold ministry leadership gifts from Ephesians 4:11-13 are notably missing whenever the church loses its way, and the three are always present when the church lives its missional vocation. The critical gifts for a missional church are apostle, prophet, and evangelist. The other two gifts are pastor and teacher:

> The gifts he gave were that some would be apostles, some prophets, some evangelists, some pastors and teachers, to equip the saints for the work of ministry, for building up the body of Christ, until all of us come to the unity of the faith and of the knowledge of the Son of God, to maturity, to the measure of the full stature of Christ.

By *missional* I mean "sent out." That is what the root word *mission* means. The Greek word for missional Christian, found in the New Testament, is *apostle.* An apostle is a "sent out" person. A missional church is one that understands itself as God's people who are gathered, blessed, gifted, and sent out. A missional church has an identity rooted in participation in God's evangelistic work in the world.

Of the five-fold ministries listed in Ephesians, the apostles, prophets, and evangelists are essential for church planting. Apostles are those who are most energized by being with people outside of the church in order to develop new faith communities.

Baughman: I love the way she defines *apostle.* I feel like it sums up so much of my calling and that of a lot of church planters. It leaves me wondering about the mission of the UMC. Is it enough to make "disciples of Jesus Christ"? Shouldn't we be making apostles who take the church's mission and inspire others to do so as well?

Their gifts include an entrepreneurial ability combined with vision and leadership to develop new communities. Paul the Apostle is a good example of this. Paul went to new locations, planted new churches with his team of friends, raised up leaders, and then moved on. People with apostolic gifts usually are not called to stay for the long haul with the new faith communities they plant. Their gifts have to do with planting and raising up leaders. There are exceptions to this rule, of course. Rev. Adam Hamilton is a notable exception within the United Methodist Church. His apostolic gift is combined with teaching and pastoral gifts, making it possible for him to remain for many years with the church he planted, United Methodist Church of the Resurrection in Leawood, Kansas.

Prophets are persons who call the church to awareness of brokenness and injustice in the world. Prophets motivate the church to get out of itself and into the world to bring the gospel to people, because salvation is not just for heaven someday but is for how we live on earth now. Prophets often irritate the church because they can seem negative and relentless in telling the church go and be the church where people suffer from injustice.

> **Jacobs:** I think Elaine is right on point. It can be so easy for the church to sit around and become comfortable when we should remain active and relevant. Prophets call us to move out of our comfort zones, and they keep before us issues we would rather not talk about or deal with.

Prophets also tell the church when it is being hypocritical and forsaking its call. A good example of a prophet in the Bible is Amos. A contemporary example is Jim Wallis, founder of Sojourners in Washington, DC.

Evangelists are gifted with the ability to communicate the gospel in word and action in ways that are winsome and compelling, inviting people into relationship with Christ. True evangelists embody the message they carry. Like prophets and apostles, evangelists are irritating to a comfort-addicted church because they are never satisfied to remain within the walls of the church, focused on the internal concerns of the established church.

> **Jacobs:** One of the signs of a dying church is when we have a "let's remain within the four walls of the church" mentality.

Their vision and call always compel them to take the church beyond itself into the world with the Good News of God's love.

These three gifts—apostle, prophet, and evangelist—are essential within a congregation for the congregation to be a multiplying, or church planting, congregation.

> **Hall:** In our experience at Urban Village Church, though it takes some work to create a congregational culture that values these three "forgotten" gifts, once you have stoked the embers consistently for a while, this new apostolic-evangelical-prophetic cultural fire begins to grow and feeds itself in a mysterious way. The Residency/Internship program at Urban Village trains young lay, clergy, and future clergy leaders to plant new things and focuses almost exclusively on uncovering these three forgotten gifts (in themselves and/or in the communities that they are gathering). The process is combustible. In five years we have trained more than thirty leaders, 30 percent of whom have gone on to plant new faith communities in diverse neighborhoods across the United States. People are hungry to experience this dynamic way of ministry.

Like other spiritual gifts (see 1 Cor. 12 for a more extensive list), these are usually combined into a "gift mix" in persons. I already noted the example of Adam Hamilton's gift mix.

We must recognize, celebrate, and equip people for leadership who have apostolic, prophetic, and evangelistic gifts if we are to be a church that bears the gospel into the world in compelling and Jesus-like ways. Lacking these essential outward-propelling gifts, the church inevitably turns in upon itself. Before long the church board meeting is focused on chicken recipes for the church dinner so as to raise the maximum amount of funds from outsiders, to pay the church's internal bills.

Here is where we need a dose of biblical literalism. The role of pastors and teachers (and some scholars say this should be a hyphenated word, pastor-teacher) is primarily to equip the church for its ministry, including its apostolic, prophetic, and evangelistic work. Equipping involves teaching the persons how to use their gifts responsibly and faithfully. This is done through leadership development as a core practice in the local church. As a pastor of local United Methodist congregations I held monthly leadership development meetings that focused on gift develop-ment and spiritual formation. I took people for conference train-ing events relevant to their gifts and call, read pertinent books and had conversations with persons to help them learn to use their specific gifts, created opportunities if none were available for them to use their gifts, and when possible helped them meet others or work with others with similar gifts so that they could be mentored.

Jacobs: I love this idea. We use the same model at our local church. Leadership development and spiritual gift formation is vital to the growth of the church. I make it a point to send persons to conferences and training events in order to spark creativity, see what other successful churches are doing, and hone in on gift development.

Equipping the apostles, prophets, and evangelists in a local church may require all of these measures and more.

The ministry gifts of apostles, prophets, and evangelists are to collectively bring people to genuine relationship with the living God. Once people are in relationship with God, it is the work of pastors and teachers to guide their formation and deepen discipleship, including helping the faith community continue to hear God's call to carry the gospel into the world. These five (or four if you hyphenate pastor-teacher) gifts are the essential leadership gifts of the church.

One important fact blows holes in our tidy ecclesiastic systems. None of the original, approximately 120 members of the first, newly launched church at Pentecost (Acts 1:15) were ministry professionals. Not one of them was ordained by a religious body to be a religious professional. No one went to seminary. There was no seminary except the Book of Daily Life with Jesus. Every person there was a layperson.

Jesus, God-made-flesh, Second Person of the Trinity, the original church planter was what my Kentucky mother calls "a workin' man." It is true he was a rabbi, but he was also a carpenter. Each of Jesus's inner circle of friends—Peter, James, and John—had jobs unrelated to religious leadership. The larger but still close circle of disciples, including the women who traveled with Jesus (and funded the work), were laity (Luke 8:1-3). Paul, the most eminent and prolific church planter of the New Testament, was also "a workin' man." In fact Paul supported himself bivocationally as a church planter, as part of his spiritual discipline. Although he could have expected payment for his ministry, he writes in 1 Corinthians 9:1-23 he chose not to so that he could be available to all sorts of people. He wanted everyone to know that the gift of salvation is free. He also chose bivocationality so that he would not have to rely on the good will or money of others in order to carry out his apostolic, prophetic, and evangelistic work.

> **Baughman:** One of the things I'm keenly interested in are tent-making congregations that are experimenting with alternative sources of revenue—thrift shops, coworking space, coffee shops, preschools, and more can offer alternative revenue so that a full-time pastor can still dedicate herself to pasturing a congregation that may not be able to afford the same things that a larger, more affluent congregation could.

At the end of this chapter he likens his bivocational choice to an athlete running in a disciplined manner so as to win the race, and he encourages others to do the same.

Original Methodism was almost entirely a lay movement. Yes, John Wesley was ordained, as was his brother Charles. They were Anglican priests. But the vast momentum of Methodism that led it to become the largest Christian movement in North America by the mid-nineteenth century was the class meeting—small groups of laypeople gathering weekly for spiritual and justice formation. Class meetings were led by trained laypeople. Methodism did not become the backbone of much needed social reform in nineteenth-century America because of its clergy. On the contrary, it grew because of lay-led small groups that cultivated real Jesus follow-ers. Many of the circuit riders who were part of early American Methodist culture were also laypeople. All of that missional activity was apostolic, prophetic, and evangelistic. It was largely led by laypeople, not clergy, who had jobs other than religious leadership. John Wesley demonstrates to us the role of the ordained person, which is to fully empower and deploy laity to use their God-given gifts for ministry, including planting new faith communities.

While it is never a good idea to try to slavishly reproduce a cultural phenomenon that happened hundreds of years ago in a different situation, we have much to learn from our spiritual ancestors, both the apostles and early Methodists. Here are three things we need to know *and practice* from both sets of ancestors, and from every reform movement throughout the history of the church.

1. Ministry is the work of the people, the whole body of Christ, not just the clergy.
2. Equipping the people for the work of ministry is the work of the pastor-teachers.
3. Pastor-teacher is a spiritual gift, not a career.

Toward an Ancient/Future Vision for Church Planting

Now let's turn our attention to our situation today. What would the United Methodist Church look like if it took seriously what the New Testament and our Methodist story teach about church planting and who is qualified to do it? Is it possible for us to move out of the deep morass in which we find ourselves regarding who can plant churches, how we can train planters, what counts as a church, and where the clergy fit (or do not fit) into this mix?

> **Jacobs:** I see what Elaine is saying, although I do believe that new church planters have a certain wiring that others do not have. Not just any clergy or layperson can start a new church. The wiring has to be there.

The answer is not easy, but it is very simple.

The first step is to come to our senses regarding our starting place for planting churches. If we start with the premise that we need an ordained person who requires a full-time salary and benefits to plant the church, we are going to be in trouble. In this model the church plant is expected to launch its first official worship gathering with two hundred regular attenders, because it takes an average of two hundred in worship to support the salary and benefits of a full-time elder.

Hall: In addition, problematic is the fact that in many conferences (regional areas) of the The United Methodist Church, there are confusing double standards about what number of people makes a "legitimate" faith community. For example, a new faith community must have 120–140 members in order to charter, or become, an "official church" in many conferences. When the median membership of congregations in most conferences is significantly less than that (fifty to seventy-five, depending on the conference), the 120–140 requirement reflects an understandable but unhelpful idealism rooted in nostalgia, not reality. I wonder if accepting and even norming that most new (and existing) faith communities will be smaller might counterintuitively free lay and clergy planters to try bold, innovative things.

If we insist on this model of plant we have to impose a short timeline for the pastor to develop the new church, usually within three years, because the Conference has to carry the expense of the pastor during the first few years of development. This type of church plant costs annual conferences around $250,000. Since most new churches today can take up to eight years to become fruitful,[4] the likelihood of this type of plant succeeding is quite small. This model is also a poor choice if the plant is going to take place in communities where there is significant poverty because even with two hundred worshippers the congregation may not be able to afford a full-time pastor's salary and benefits. In this scenario, which has tended to dominate our method of planting in recent decades, the starting point for planting unwittingly shifts away from apostolic call toward making sure the ordained pastor (who is guaranteed a full-time salary and benefits according to our polity) has the mandated salary and benefits.

If on the other hand we begin with Jesus and the gospel, following his example and teaching, practicing everything that has been said thus far about ministry (including planting) as the work of the people, we have exciting times ahead. If we focus on developing the laity who have planting gifts and deploying them in teams of two to five people to start new faith communities beyond the walls of the church, there are endless opportunities to plant. The "why" of planting must always be that Jesus told us to make disciples.

> **Jacobs:** Clearly Elaine is onto something very powerful. I'm not sure it would be as effective in my context where African Americans look to the pastor for guidance, leadership, and vision.

Next we have to sort out the "what" of planting. What constitutes a church? Must there be a church building, pews, organ, and clergy for church to be church? Not according to Jesus. He says that wherever two or three of us are gathered in his name, he is with us (Matt. 18:20). *Ekklesia,* the Greek word that we translate into English as *church*, simply means "gathering." At its simplest level church consists of two or three followers of Jesus gathered around Jesus in order to worship him and participate in his work in the world.

Decades ago when I scarcely had a high school diploma much less college or seminary degrees, when I was a young adult with two young children and had only been a Christian a few years, I began to dream of gathering people in my neighborhood to read the Bible and pray together. At the time I was not in the UMC but in a Pentecostal church. (Pentecostals, incidentally, are on the Wesleyan family tree.) In that tradition laypeople were taught to pray, teach, preach, and lead as a matter of course. Leading was all about spiritual gifts. After feeling this peculiar longing for many weeks I talked to one of the pastors on staff whose area of responsibility was disciple formation. I told her what I was feeling, but expressed hesitance to start a group in my neighborhood, because my family and I were going to move in the next few months, and I was young and didn't know what I was doing. Very wisely she said, "Follow what your heart is asking you to do. Even if you only meet with your neighbors a few times, God will work through that to bless them and to bless you. Leave the outcome to God."

> **Hall:** This is deep spiritual wisdom! "Leave the outcome to God" is an idea that probably 100 percent of Christian leaders would agree with but far fewer actually practice. I know that, especially at the beginning of planting, I was living at the other end of the spectrum: I was working as if the outcome was totally dependent on me and my effectiveness. It was only the practice of contemplative prayer that helped (and continues to help) me to move toward the practice of "leaving the outcome to God." We've often heard the maxim, "Work as if everything depended on you and pray as if everything depended on God." But what if, as Richard Rohr asks, we embraced the alternative of "Work as if everything depended on God and pray as if everything depended on you"?

So I did. I knocked on the doors of persons on both sides of the street within six houses of mine. I had no idea what I was doing and did not feel that I had any expertise. I was and am an introvert. This harebrained idea stretched me to the limit. But the longing to gather neighbors was persistent and the pastor urged me to do it.

A small handful of women came to the group, which lasted a whopping six weeks and then my family and I moved. What was gained from this experience? Only God knows the full outcome, but for those weeks it was a taste of heaven for me and for my neighbors. We laughed, talked, read the Bible, and prayed for each other. Our preschool-aged children played in the basement under supervision of the woman that we hired to take care of them. During that time we offered each other friendship and support that lasted long after I moved away.

That experience was my first foray into missional church planting, although no one called it that in 1983. I myself would not have called it church planting, because there was no building, pastor, pews, or program. My heart knew at some level that this sort of neighborhood engagement was part of what I was born to do, although the ecclesiology I had been formed in would not have called that gathering a church. Even so, that ecclesiology did empower me to begin to explore my gifts and experience my call as a layperson.

A year later the pastor who initially encouraged me to start the neighborhood group asked me to lead an ongoing women's group she had started several years previously. With fear and trembling I finally agreed to do it. This time the group included about twelve women who were seeking a deeper walk with Christ. The group was called Dayspring and included worship, teaching, prayer, and table fellowship. After I took the pastor's place in leading the group half of them stopped coming, because they were pastor groupies, but within a few weeks the remaining group doubled with new people and eventually grew to about forty. I developed a team of women whom I asked to help me lead. When we gathered, I would teach for twenty minutes then divide the group into smaller groups, which my team members facilitated. In the small groups participants discussed questions about the teaching and prayed for one another, which took about forty-five minutes. We also took care of group members between times, praying, staying in touch, helping with each other's kids, and providing meals for one another when there was sickness or hospitalization.

My teaching focus that whole year was what it means to be a follower of Jesus, including both a life of prayer and a life of compassion and justice. I did not use the words *apostolic*, *prophetic*, *evangelistic* to describe what I was doing, because they would not have occurred to me at the time. But looking back those are precisely the gifts I was exercising.

At the end of the year, five of the women asked me to baptize them because they had been evangelized by the process of our year together. That is, they had experienced the Holy Spirit calling them to follow Jesus, and they had begun to follow Jesus over that year. I asked the pastor of discipleship to come and assist me in baptizing them, and she was happy to help. We baptized them in the swimming pool at my house. Please note—she, a professionally trained pastor, a full-time clergy person, assisted me, a layperson, in baptizing people I had evangelized and discipled for a year.

All of these developments happened when I was a layperson with a high school education. I even served Communion at times in Dayspring, and we all experienced genuine grace mediated through this sacrament. I was able to serve Communion because in that tradition we believed that ministry is the work of all the people. To be a Christian was to have the authority of Christ to do whatever was being asked by the Holy Spirit. We did not believe sacramental authority was limited to clergy. It was part of being a baptized Christian.

Hall: Yes! What Elaine is suggesting in this chapter is not just a shift of approach or strategy but an invitation to think again about things like sacramental authority. If laypeople are called to plant and pastor communities, is it possible that they might also be called to help those new communities celebrate the sacraments? This is not to suggest that *every* layperson is called to celebrate sacraments—this is not an "equal rights" argument—but that

perhaps the charisms of order and sacrament are deeply connected. So if a layperson is asked by God to gather and organize a
new community for mission (what *order* actually means), wouldn't
it follow that God *might* ask that same person to baptize the new
followers and spread the table of Eucharist with the community
she had gathered in?

Before I proceed further, let me say that I have been a United
Methodist for more than twenty years, and I have always complied
with my denomination's practice regarding sacramental authority, especially since becoming involved in helping others to start
missional communities beyond the walls of the church. There are
several very workable paths for United Methodists, Lutherans, and
others for whom sacramental authority is reserved for ordained
clergy, to make the sacraments available for congregations planted
and led by teams of laypeople. This is not a real obstacle to laypersons planting and leading new faith communities.

Was Dayspring a church? Some people in the United Methodist
world would think it was not, because we didn't gather on Sunday,
it wasn't led by a clergy person, and there was no pressure on the
people who came to formally join the "main" church that anchored
the ministry.

Jacobs: I love this idea. If we want to reach more people then we
must offer powerful experiences on days outside of Sunday.

(My team and I held a kingdom of God rather than denominational
mindset though I did not have language to name it as such, at
the time.) Looking back I know Dayspring was a church. Today I
would call it a missional church anchored at the larger congregation where I was a member. Dayspring had every element of what

it means to be the gathered, worshipping, serving, missional body of Christ. We even celebrated the sacraments. This church was led by laity, not because clergy were unavailable but because in our Pentecostal theology, ministry was understood to flow from the gifts of the people. Our theological starting point was the call and gifts of the Holy Spirit, not someone's professional role in ministry.

This is a long and autobiographical way of saying that I know from firsthand, pre-Methodist experience that every gift of the Holy Spirit is available and given to people regardless of clergy and lay distinctions. Apostolic, prophetic, and evangelistic gifts enabling teams to plant and lead new faith communities are given to many laypeople who are just waiting for a pastor to call forth the gifts and equip them. That is precisely what my pastor did all those years ago. She exercised her teaching, preaching, and caring gifts in a way that called forth my and other people's gifts for ministry. She fanned into flame the apostolic, prophetic, and evangelistic gifts of myself and other people. She did not see our gifts as a threat to her authority or identity. On the contrary, we were her pride and joy.

Jacobs: This reminds me a lot of what we do at our church. Pastors should never feel threatened to open the pulpit to others with a relevant word. At our local church our laypersons are equipped and trained to speak on Sunday mornings. It is always a powerful experience to see others grow spiritually and it gives me a needed break.

So is it possible for us to follow these biblical and Wesleyan practices in the UMC today? Absolutely. During the past decade, most of my academic research and my own on-the-ground practice of ministry has focused on equipping and empowering laypeople within and beyond the UMC to launch and lead new kinds of faith communities in diverse places. With my former student Rev. Dr.

Larry Duggins, I founded the Missional Wisdom Foundation, which is a collection of diverse learning communities that help the church imagine and embrace a lively future with a fully equipped and deployed laity. (For more about the Missional Wisdom Foundation and its training programs, see www.missionalwisdom.com.) Seven years ago in response to my students' desire to learn how to plant faith communities beyond the walls of the church, I launched two kinds of missional faith communities with students. These communities, called New Day and the Epworth Project, continue and have multiplied. They are led by teams of laypersons for the most part and have become important ministry models impacting the imagination of the United Methodist Church and other mainline denominations nationally and around the world. The model of New Day is very similar to Dayspring, which I described earlier. Communities like New Day can be anchored in established churches, led by teams of laypeople who are nurtured by clergy from the anchor church.

As I travel extensively to teach, preach, and help the church reawaken to its apostolic vocation, I encounter increasing numbers of Christians and innovative faith communities that have reclaimed the five gifts of leadership and are taking church beyond the walls of church buildings. They are also retrieving the ancient wisdom that we are called to bear the gospel into the world because we are participants in the kingdom of God. I am excited and full of hope because of their example.

Hall: This whole chapter just fills me with joy and hope. If I had to put my money on one ethos/approach/strategy for the future of Christianity (thank God I don't have to, because our mission in the future can and should include multiple and diverse strategies), it would be what Elaine is passionately offering here. It is one of those rare approaches that can be faithfully applied in *every* context—rural, urban, suburban; Deep South, West Coast, Midwest, Northeast; etc.

Questions about who can and should serve Communion and baptize people in lay planted and led communities are easily addressed. The more challenging question has to do with how we understand the role of a full-time, paid clergy person. In the years ahead there will be fewer full-time clergy. Because of economic necessity we will increasingly need to rely on bivocational pastors. For missional purposes, though, cultivating teams of several bivocational leaders makes much more sense than limiting leadership to ordained clergy. The key to successfully navigating this shift will not be a fight about sacramental authority but submission to the clear teaching of scripture and our own Methodist beginnings. The work of the people is ministry. The work of the clergy is to equip people for ministry. If we can adopt that understanding as we educate and send out ordained, paid clergy, we will see exciting years ahead. In this scenario seminary graduates will be prepared to serve in a pastoral role that combines teaching, spiritual direction, community organizing, and encouragement. The paid clergy person will, among other things, function as a leader to the lead teams of multiple missional faith communities led by teams of laypeople.

As Christendom continues to decline in the United States, the need for thoroughly equipped, called, and gifted laypersons to plant and lead the church cannot be overstated. The future of the United Methodist Church will rise or fall based upon how we equip, deploy, and trust laypeople. This state of affairs is not a bad thing. It is a return to God's original intent for the Body of Christ.

Truly Multiethnic Churches Don't Work

DOUG CUNNINGHAM, NEW DAY CHURCH

You have heard it said . . .

I grew up in suburban Ohio attending a large, mostly white United Methodist church. When I was in high school, our church youth group traveled to the Appalachian Mountain region of North Carolina for a mission trip. I was shocked by the rural poverty, fascinated by the variety of Appalachian cultures, and inspired to spend two weeks as part of a faith community that was reaching out to connect with new people and situations.

I had my first major Christian conversion during that trip, setting me on a path toward ordained ministry and igniting a hunger to engage with life beyond the comfort and privilege of my hometown. This passion grew when I attended seminary and found meaningful relationships with people across lines of race and sexual orientation. Then a term as a missionary in the Philippines further connected me to the richness of the wider world. I wondered why relating with the marvelous variety of the human family was

---

Doug Cunningham is the founding pastor for New Day Church in New York, New York. ◆ newdaybronx.org

not a more common experience in our church. The Gospels tell many stories of Jesus crossing ethnic boundaries to connect with Samaritans, a Syro-Phoenician woman, and Gentiles. Why then is the United Methodist Church in the United States so racially homogenous?

In a nation that is 64 percent white, 16 percent Latino, 12.3 percent black, and 4.7 percent Asian, the United Methodist Church is 94 percent white, 2 percent Latino, 2 percent black, and 1 percent Asian.[1] Individual congregations rarely cross racial boundaries. Out of 32,608 United Methodist churches in the United States, less than 2 percent reported in 2009 that at least 20 percent of their folks were of a different racial group than the majority.[2]

Ross: This should be shocking.

In 2007 I experienced a clear and persistent call to start a new congregation that would challenge this trend and establish a boundary-crossing congregation. As I began reading books and attending church planting conferences, I was impressed by the spirit of innovation I encountered among church planters. I was surprised, however, to find that this innovative culture expressed little interest in challenging the church's lack of diversity. The primary focus seemed to be new and creative ways to reach as many people as possible. Many argue that the best way to do that is to stay in one's ethnic and cultural comfort zone.

Ed Stetzer, a popular author, speaker, and church growth expert, stated at a national multicultural ministry conference in 2013 that "multicultural ministry is a recipe for conflict." He continued, "It's simply a statistical reality that when everyone thinks similarly, they can engage others more quickly and more effectively and churches will grow."[3] Best-selling author and church planter Rick Warren of Saddleback Church in California agrees. In his classic book, *The Purpose Driven Church*, Warren writes, "The easiest people for you to reach for Christ are those who are most like you."[4]

It may be easier to reach large numbers in a racially and culturally homogenous ministry, but if thousands of people gather in predominantly white churches that simply perpetuate the racial dynamics we find in the wider society, how will the ministry prepare people to challenge discrimination and build diversity emblematic of the reign of God?

Harrison: It won't. It hasn't. We have seen that.

Not every congregation needs to be multiethnic. In particular, I realize the importance of the black church in this country. In the 1800s, black congregants who were unwilling to tolerate racial discrimination in white churches walked out to form their own congregations. Today, in the midst of ongoing racism and violence, the black church, as well as African, Caribbean, Latino, and Asian churches, can be critically important centers of healing and empowerment. At the same time, multiethnic congregations, when they challenge racial discrimination in the church and society, offer ways to embody the boundary-crossing ministry of Jesus. This was our aim in starting New Day Church.

But I say to you . . .

From the beginning my daughter, Lisa, has been a key partner in planting New Day and developing our church's vision. When I discussed with her the importance of diversity, she helped me see that inclusion alone is not enough. She is mixed race (I'm white, and my wife is Filipino). Through the years of my ministry, we lived and worshiped in a variety of suburban and urban settings. She generally felt included but not empowered in the ministry of these churches. She asked, "Isn't the gospel calling us to more than inclusion?"

Too often inclusion involves a dominant culture deciding to invite members of other races, classes, cultures, or sexual orientations to join, without making significant changes in that dominant culture.

> **Baughman:** This happens with dominant generations as well. I've seen many churches say they want younger generations to be a part of the church without making changes or empowering younger generations to lead beyond token representatives.

A recent study conducted by three universities has found that despite racial diversity in congregations, "the dominant white racial frames may go unchallenged."[5] "Whose interests are multiracial congregations serving?" asked researcher Kevin Dougherty, PhD, associate professor of sociology in Baylor's College of Arts and Sciences. "We want to believe that they promote a shared, integrated identity for all. But the truth may be that many are advancing a form of Anglo-conformity instead."[6]

> **Ross:** When I started Christ's Foundry, I did not even know the Spanish songs that we should be singing. Finding persons from the cultures I was seeking to reach who had a pulse on good music from those cultures was essential for our worship repertoire.

How do we move beyond a diversity that conforms to the norms of the dominant culture? At New Day we are intentionally building a boundary-crossing congregation where no one group dominates. As Lisa describes it: "In the act of crossing boundaries we assume responsibility to meet people where they are, we confront the injustice of the boundary itself and the process transforms us."[7]

This practice is at the heart of the ministry of Jesus who had theological conversations with women and ministered with Gentiles and Samaritans in ways that challenged common prejudices and practices in his society and among the religious authorities (John 4:1-42; Mark 5:1-20, 7:24-37, 8:1-10, 14:3-9; Luke 10:25-37). If Jesus challenged the discrimination of his day, we believe that we are called to challenge it in our society.

The Right Leadership

Our first task was to build a leadership team that was LGBTQ and straight, male and female; and black, white, Latino, Asian, and mixed race. We spoke Spanish, English, and Tagalog. We covered a wide span of ages, from the twenties on up. We have made the principle of boundary-crossing a top priority in every ministry decision we make from selecting leaders to planning worship.

> **Harrison:** I found myself in a very multicultural situation in prison that seminary didn't prepare me for.

Through the years of my ministry, I have learned that the only effective way to challenge social boundaries is with clear intention and persistence. In 1997 I was appointed to a predominantly white congregation in a mostly black neighborhood. The demographics in the neighborhood were changing rapidly, due to white flight.

We needed to clarify what we believed God was calling us to do and be in that neighborhood. After much discussion, we decided at a church council meeting to become a multiracial church. Once the vision was clear, we elected some new church leaders who were committed to the new vision. We initiated several bold changes, which drew some negative reactions from longtime members, but also generated a lot of positive energy as we moved toward our vision. One was establishing Spirit Chorus, a new multiracial and intergenerational gospel/contemporary praise choir, which sang once a month. It was a big hit and gave the congregation a regular experience of seeing and being uplifted by our vision. I was encouraged one day at the seniors' weekly lunch to overhear an older white woman saying to her husband, "We can't go out of town that weekend, that's the Sunday the Spirit Chorus sings." Another step forward was the decision of a dynamic young black man named Chuck to lead our men's group. He initiated conversations with the current members and invited a lot of new men to join. Our first Men's Sunday was a multiracial worship celebration that packed the house.

Starting New Day Church from scratch provided the opportunity to create a boundary-crossing ministry from the beginning. We determined, for example, that every worship service would include music from a variety of cultural and ethnic traditions. This was not about culturally appropriating the music of other ethnicities but about worshipping in a variety of ways that spoke authentically to the variety of folks in the room.

> **Ross:** I appreciate the emphasis is on worship and not on simply seeking to be diverse for diversity's sake. Finding the root meanings of songs from various cultures offers new and deeper understandings of the God we worship. Lord knows how my understanding of God has been deepened through cross-cultural influences.

Our worship team spends hours each week not only rehearsing songs but discussing the impact and meaning of various songs. The team has had emotional, challenging, and sometimes funny conversations about which songs to sing during Sunday worship. I remember discussing a song with a line about Jesus "riding on the clouds."[8] For some of our worship team members this line evoked a powerful image of the healing presence of God, while others couldn't get past a literal picture of Jesus in the clouds. We are reminded that differences are often shaped by our experiences growing up in and out of church.

> **Harrison:** And these new ways of seeing and understanding overflow into other areas of our lives.

These conversations help build trust in the worship team, empowering them to lead the congregation boldly in worship. One Sunday, one of our worship team members was overwhelmed by an experience of the Holy Spirit and began running around the sanctuary. This was not a familiar sight for some in our church, but his willingness to respond authentically to his worship experience helped create an environment where other worshipers can be more open to the Spirit in whatever ways are genuine for them. Our goal is for each of us to connect with God authentically, whether that be quietly or with physical expression, and to be open to what is authentic for others.

Confronting Injustice

A boundary-crossing congregation moves beyond people with differences sitting in the same room together for worship. It is also important to challenge the injustice of the way these boundaries divide us. In February 2012, New York City police officers burst into the Bronx home of a black teenager named Ramarley Graham, whom they suspected of possessing marijuana. They shot and killed the unarmed teen in his apartment in front of his grandmother and three-year-old brother.[9]

Following the shooting, I joined several other ministers in meeting with the Bronx Commander for the New York City Police

Department. We went one by one around the table expressing our deep concerns about this incident. Almost all of the black and Latino pastors shared a personal story of being stopped and harassed by the police. None of the white ministers had had the same experience. And once again, the bubble of unconsidered privilege that so often surrounds me as a white man was burst by hearing the experiences of others. For the police to kill a teen in such a manner would have been unthinkable in the white suburban community where I grew up. Several of my high school classmates bought and sold marijuana, but the idea that the police would follow one of them home, burst through the door, and shoot them in their living room is hard to imagine. Yet this was the reality that black and brown teens face in my church's neighborhood.

When it became clear that the New York City police officers who killed Ramarley Graham and another unarmed black man named Eric Garner would not face prosecution, a number of our members participated in a march in the south Bronx urging our city to curb police violence aimed particularly at black and brown men and women.

In addition to confronting injustice out in the world, a boundary-crossing congregation is also committed to supporting one another in our own process of being transformed. Essential to this is building relationships. We provide conversation circles during worship to increase opportunities for people to get to know one another across boundaries.

Baughman: This is a risk, but well worth it. As soon as you put people into conversation circles during worship (which we do weekly at Union), the preacher loses control of the message. Sometimes, people get offended in these conversations. I've found that is when I take on the role of "pastor" in the pulpit that teaches a flock how to talk to one another in the face of passionate disagreement.

We offer small group conversations outside of worship on the Bible, prayer, and books like Michelle Alexander's *The New Jim Crow* to discuss faith and social issues from our different perspectives. We must be able to bring all of who we are, share our stories, and listen to each other. It's so easy to retreat into our own worldview.

> **Harrison:** I am afraid that I make the trip into my own worldview far too often! Sometimes it is so painful to hear and acknowledge the stories of others but it is necessary.

It's hard to question assumptions we've grown up with in order to build authentic, caring relationships with people across boundaries, but this effort is necessary to build solidarity in a multiethnic setting.

> **Ross:** I have personally experienced and witnessed how social justice action is almost always born from these personal transformations that take place through persons' relationships with God and others, especially from diverse backgrounds.

Open and Affirming Is More Than a Slogan on the Church Sign

We have likewise experimented with ways to deepen our conversations about sexual orientation and gender identity. A group of gay men in our church began meeting with one of our ministers in 2012. They discussed faith and sexuality in ways that were healing and liberating for them. At the end of the series, several group members wanted to bring the conversation to the rest of the congregation. So they proposed that we establish a Queer Liberation Series in which they would plan and lead all the worship services in that month. They would bring in speakers, show film clips, act in dramatic skits, lead us in singing, and pray in ways that would invite the entire congregation into these important conversations.

The series felt like a radical move at the time. Reared in the traditions of the United Methodist clergy, being asked to give over several Sundays in a row to any group felt like a challenge to my pastoral authority. And yet, as I listened to the group, I began to realize the greater importance of ending the silencing of LGBTQ voices in the church. They designated one Sunday to focus on HIV-AIDS and another on gender. The first Sunday in the series was titled: Coming Out, Authenticity as a Path to Power. This became an experience of "coming out" for the whole congregation as we crossed conversation boundaries of sexual orientation and gender identity.

As time drew near for this first service I was both nervous and excited. On that Sunday morning, as I was preparing for worship, I noticed that I had missed a call from my bishop. Then one of our district superintendents walked into our worship space, then another. In a few minutes others came in and then the bishop. He had brought the entire cabinet for our coming-out Sunday! During the service I was curious about how the experience was affecting them. The bishop seemed enthusiastic, and I had the sense that several of the district superintendents were also moved.

The service started with a gripping testimony from one of our leaders, who shared his journey of coming to full acceptance of himself as a gay man. He talked about the pain of being in the closet and having to hide an important part of who he was. His words were moving for many in the congregation who had often witnessed his spiritual wisdom and pastoral gifts. After a time of prayer we sang a song with a driving beat and lyrics that reminded us that no matter what we are going through, God has not forgotten us. Suddenly people began praising God, crying and shouting in an outpouring of the Spirit anointing us as a boundary-crossing church.

In his teaching about love, Jesus highlights the compassion of a Samaritan—a member of an ethnic, cultural, and religious group that Jews often disrespected. Jesus wasn't saying that the dominant group should be charitable and generous toward such marginalized groups. Rather, he was teaching us that the ones we marginalize may be the ones who teach us how to love.

Ross: Powerful insight. At Christ's Foundry we once declined the offer of a suburban church to do a soccer clinic for our children and instead our youth held a soccer clinic for the suburban children. This was a very transformative day for the Christ's Foundry youth and for the suburban children.

In discriminating against LGBTQ folks in the church, straight people miss out on great opportunities to expand our understanding of the broad spectrum of human sexual orientation and gender identity. This growing awareness has helped me understand and embrace my own masculinity, moving beyond stereotypical limitations to realize that I can be masculine in a whole variety of ways. I was intrigued and moved, for example, when a tall, muscular, black gay man in our congregation read a poem in which he referred to his masculinity as "elegant."

Straight people in faith communities are not called to include LGBTQ folks out of the goodness of their inclusive hearts, as if straight people were the gatekeepers of the faith! Rather authentic boundary crossing helps the whole church realize the treasure LGBTQ persons are already bringing into the life of the church, inspiring all of us to come out and be our authentic selves.

Baughman: This paragraph is critical to ministry with those who have been marginalized. One of our best recent sermons (led by several community members) focused on what the church and rising generations have to learn from the gay community. It was an incredible night, but the subject is a little misleading. We've been learning from the gay community in our ministry from day one.

Strengthening Our Model

These rich experiences have helped build a faith community
that embraces both our differences and similarities. One area of
weakness in our ministry model has been the reality that a white
straight male has been the pastor for the entire life of the congregation. No matter how much boundary crossing we do, it will be
hard for us to fulfill our purpose as a boundary-crossing congregation when the one full-time pastor represents the most dominant demographic perspective.

One day that will change. In the meantime, I am mentoring
several gifted and committed leaders in our congregation, many
of them people of color, in preaching, teaching, pastoral care, and
other areas of leadership. We have formed a Community of the
Word that meets regularly to prepare ten lay preachers in our congregation who have now delivered a total of seventeen sermons.

> **Ross:** This reminds me of Psalm 145:4: "Each generation will praise
> you and tell the next generation about the great things you do."

I have provided them with some basic teaching in biblical interpretation and exegesis. Each time we assign someone a
date to preach, they bring their sermon first to the Community
of the Word. The feedback they receive from the group has been
immensely helpful in their process of preparing powerful sermons. Two of those preachers are now in seminary and others
have talked about enrolling. Two of them have also now taken on
part-time pastoral positions in our church.

We have made it a priority at New Day to encourage one another
to find and live into our calling. Our discipleship system, at this
point, includes two courses. Growing in Faith 101 is an introduc-
tion to the ministry of Jesus, the New Testament, the principles of

our church, and what it means to be a member. Growing in Faith 201 invites participants to explore their purpose. We focus on the calling of Moses and particularly on the two central questions of Exodus 3: Who am I? (3:11) and Who is God? (3:13-15).

The question Who am I? is about my gifts, my passion, and any anxiety I may have about embracing my calling. When Moses asks, "Who am I to go to Pharaoh?" we see his fear that he might not be capable of doing what God is calling him to do. Those who are called often experience a sense of unworthiness. Just as Isaiah responded to his call by saying, "I am a man of unclean lips," so we often feel unworthy to do what we believe God is calling us to. And yet we realize that throughout the scriptures and all around us, God is calling ordinary people to great things.

This sense of unworthiness that is our natural response to the holiness of God can be complicated and confused by the discrimination that still runs through the church. At New Day we affirm that the calling of God is for all people across boundaries including race, class, sexual orientation, gender, and age. One of our New Day young adult leaders made a speech at a national United Methodist gathering. A bishop in attendance spoke with him afterward about considering seminary and ordination, but he shared with the bishop that as a gay man, he was not interested in hiding who God has created him to be in order to survive the church's ordination process.

> **Harrison:** So his voice is silenced even as he is being affirmed by a bishop and called to lift his voice by the one who created him!

Encouraging all of our congregants to embrace the calling of God is an important part of becoming a *ministry of all believers*. We are moving into new territory, making mistakes but also experiencing breakthroughs, as we seek to live into all that God is calling us to be. We are inviting many who have been hurt or excluded by the church into a stronger relationship with God through a faith community that affirms them and their calling. And we want to partner with others who are also following Jesus in the boundary-crossing movement of God.

New Church Starts with African American Community Aren't Sustainable

DEREK JACOBS, THE VILLAGE UNITED METHODIST CHURCH

You have heard it said . . .

Over the years, I have spent many hours sitting in conference meetings, had numerous side conversations with colleagues, and read many articles. I've seen the statistics focused on the decline of the African American Church in United Methodism. Yes, it is not a secret that the African American Church is in decline. It has been for quite some time. I am getting tired of always talking about it, though. Who wants to come to a church where all you hear about is death? I contend it would be more beneficial for us to spend less time talking about decline and more time coming up with and implementing creative solutions to the problem.

Derek Jacobs is the founding pastor for The Village United Methodist Church in DeSoto, Texas. ◆ thevillageumc.org

> **Baughman:** I've hit that point in conversations about the decline of mainline denominations. I'm much more intrigued by generative conversations that explore our potential.

But I say to you . . .

I strongly believe that the way to turn the statistics around and begin to grow is by creating new, relevant faith communities in mission fields with a high concentration of African Americans and the potential of even more growth. A planter myself, what I love about starting new faith communities is the fact that we are not confined by an established regime that either wants to stay where we have been or go back into Egypt. Launching new faith communities gives us the opportunity to take risks and do church in innovative ways that encourage sustainability. I serve as lead pastor at The Village United Methodist Church in Desoto, Texas, a predominantly African American faith community near Dallas. The Village was chartered as a fully incorporated United Methodist Church on April 14, 2013. We were the first North Texas Conference church to charter in many years. We are so very humbled and grateful for this opportunity. Many church plants have failed, but it was time for a success story especially in the predominantly African American context, and God chose The Village. The pastoral staff and gifted laity of The Village have simply been open to trying new things and doing church in ways that go against the norm. I strongly believe, based on my experience, the model for new African American faith communities and even existing congregations includes a much shorter worship celebration, a team approach to worship design and church leadership, flawless hospitality, and an effective strategy for financial support.

> **Brown:** If we had to do it all over again, I would be extremely focused on the church's financial sustainability.

One Hour of Power

When we were planning and preparing to launch, the length of the worship service was a major focus. A large percentage of the core group had the DNA of our mother church, and they were accustomed to a two-hour experience. As we sat around the meeting table in various homes in our mission field, we began to throw around ideas about doing something different, something that would not be considered the norm for a predominantly African American church. This led us to a close and deep look at who lived in and was moving into our mission field.

As a result of our time and demographic studies, it became clear that our current and potential mission field was primarily young families. We had a core group of young families who we knew we had to reach and retain our primary target audience. But how? From many conversations we knew our target audience is addicted to the fast life. We want what we want, and we want it now. If we want to contact someone, we can send them an instant message by texting, tweeting, or posting on Facebook. If we are hungry, we can microwave an entire meal in two minutes. When our driver's license expires, we renew it online within seconds. Forget standing in line at the bank when we can deposit our paycheck with a smartphone and have it in our account instantly. We want things fast. Our attention spans have shortened.

Every Sunday we are competing with so many activities that we have to give the people in the congregation a reason to come to church and stay tuned in to the experience. Years ago, Sunday morning schedules were not as jam-packed as they have become today. When I was growing up and when my parents were growing up, Sunday morning was simply church. Now we are competing with all of the activities our children are involved in. So why even compete? We don't want people to choose between going to church and doing something else on the list. Why not establish a model where we can do it all? In addition, many of our young people today have a sour taste about church and think church is boring.

> **Brown:** In some cases, church *is* boring, but not at the Village!

They do not feel like they get anything out of the experience. Some people have commented that church is so boring not even God tunes in. We are striving to break this type of thinking and change it by offering a fun, exciting, and challenging experience.

There was no question: we were going to implement the one-hour worship experience at The Village and stick to it. I remember when we told people who were not part of the core group about our decision. Many people told us, "A two-hour service is the way it has always been in the African American Church and changing to one hour will never work." Being a fierce competitor, these comments made me even more determined to prove that it can be done and it is indeed sustainable in an African American context.

> **Baughman:** Every innovative church planter is told time and time again how their plans won't work. While this can be discouraging, sometimes it pushes us in just the right way.

We began to flesh out exactly how the one-hour service would flow. Part of our work included visiting other African American churches and observing exactly what could be cut out of worship while still offering a powerful experience. We learned that much of what took place in worship just went too long. Over the course of the worship celebration, we could tell people were becoming less engaged as they began looking around and checking the time on their watches. Congregational and choir singing went too long. The prayer was too long. The sermon was definitely too long. The announcements were too long and could be cut out altogether.

> **Jacobs:** I believe we are very smart people and God has blessed us with the ability to read, so why not scroll the announcements on the screens before worship, during the offering, after worship, or disseminate the announcements during the week via social media?

As a result of our church visits, we decided to time everything we do in worship. This requires more preparation and rehearsal by the worship team, but it has proved worth the sacrifice. We require all people on the worship team to rehearse and time what they have been charged to do. We rehearse the prayer, the music, and the sermon.

> **Rangel:** My experience is that people are not trained well in what they should say in worship. Derek made a wise move in training his leadership to know what to say in order to create, in one hour, the experience of what you would have in two or three hours of worship.

A person who grew up in the African American church might think we are not leaving room for the Holy Spirit to move. I know this is hard for some, to believe the Holy Spirit can move in a two-minute prayer, a five-minute song, and a fifteen-minute sermon.

On January 24, 2010, we launched this new faith community now known as The Village, previously the South Campus of St. Luke "Community" United Methodist Church in Dallas, Texas. We launched with a seamless one-hour worship celebration and people had a moving experience. People came up to us after worship and told us they did not feel like they missed anything. Worship did not feel rushed. The steady flow of the service eliminates downtime. Combining offering and announcements eliminates more time and works because we are used to multitasking. The preacher gives a word in fifteen minutes or less. Everything we do is designed to keep moving, to be quick and seamless, which we believe decreases the chances of a person's mind checking out. We even teach this in our Sermon Preparation Workshop every third Thursday at The Village, when appointed pastors, lay speakers, and people exploring a call to ministry come together to hone their gifts of teaching and preaching. One point we make clear and reiterate every session is the importance of hooking people quickly in order to make the message meaningful. If we fail to do that, getting their attention later becomes very difficult, if not impossible.

When I leave church I am fed, refreshed, and challenged, which proves to me that it's not about quantity. It's about quality. At The Village word of mouth has traveled fast and far that persons know they can come participate in a powerful and very moving one-hour service and not feel like they have to give up a whole day just for church. I have never heard anyone complain about how short worship celebration was.

Corporate Worship Planning

Along with a one-hour worship service, a team approach to worship design and church leadership is also vital to sustaining new African American churches. Historically, the culture in the African American church has been very top-down with the senior pastor as the main and sometimes only authority figure. When decisions need to be made or worship and programs need to be planned, many times it is the senior pastor who decides what needs to be done with little to no input from other people on the leadership team. It's almost like, "Do what I say, when I say, even if you don't agree with me." In my opinion, this model is not effective in starting and sustaining new African American churches in the twenty-first century. At The Village, the top-down approach would never work, nor would it even cross my mind. Instead, we have implemented more of a partnership model where everyone is part of the team and has a voice in determining where we go and how we get there.

I grew up United Methodist and it was tattooed on my mind at a very young age that laity and clergy are to be partners in ministry. The laity cannot do ministry effectively without the clergy, and the clergy cannot carry out ministry effectively without the laity. We all must come together as a team for the building of the kingdom of God.

> **Rangel:** John Wesley believed that we, as pastors, perfect the people of God to do the ministry, which does not end on earth but continues on in heaven. For Wesley there was no value distinction between clergy and laity; both were partners in ministry. Involving laypeople in active leadership at Casa Linda was key to our growth since finances prevented us from hiring any additional staff or clergy.

This approach has been instrumental to my ministry as a whole and to the success of The Village. We come together as a team weekly in different settings, especially places in the community where we can be seen, in order to build relationships with one another and make sure that we agree on the vision for the ministry. These relationship-building and planning sessions help us to be at our best each and every Sunday. The congregation deserves our very best, and we have one shot at it. We cannot get to Sunday, flop, and then ask for a do-over. These team-building sessions help us to communicate effectively and it allows each of us to feel safe to holding one another accountable.

These planning sessions also include a sermon critique team (made up of both men and women), which I have found are rarely seen in African American churches.

> **Baughman:** Clergy like John and Charles Wesley get a lot of the credit for the Methodist movement, but laypeople were instrumental to *everything* they did—not just as volunteers but as decision-makers, strategists, preachers, and more. Most of the successful, innovative new church starts that I know of are incredibly effective at empowering laity to make decisions and execute ministry.

I love to learn and become better at using the gifts God has blessed me with. This team offers me helpful insight on content, delivery, impact, and relevance. The team also plays a big role in helping to flesh out sermon titles, series, and illustrations, which help us to stay relevant and meet the needs of God's people. Worship is more powerful when everyone feels ownership and is on the same page.

> **Brown:** Derek's teaching in this area is so far ahead of where most churches are operating. He's leading into the future.

We have witnessed our worship experience on Sunday mornings going to the next level each and every week. Because we are intentional about team, we are able to offer persons an experience that will leave them wanting more, inspiring them to come back and get their Village fix.

> **Brown:** Although agreement is key, there are times when the leader or leaders have to make a call to get the group to the next level.

Now let me be clear: just because we have a solid team does not mean we always get along or agree with one another. We have found that it is not effective to have a lot of "yes" people on the team. We need "yes" people, "no" people, "have you thought about this" people, "we can" people, "creative" people, "risk-taking" people. Our team is very diverse, and we welcome persons on our team to challenge ideas and one another, which helps us to always flesh out the best path for the ministry. Scripture is clear in Ephesians that all of us have different gifts for the building of God's kingdom. There have been times when we have been deeply engaged in planning, and we were not all in agreement with one another. And since we believe our work is so important we will sit there and grind it out. We have found that each time we come out stronger as a team and even if we don't all agree, we are still on the same page and we move forward together.

Flawless Hospitality

As we continue to pursue our formula for sustaining new African American faith communities, flawless hospitality must be a part of our model. At The Village, we have been intentional about striving to provide this level of hospitality. We put much time in this area of ministry simply because we feel it can make or break the church. Failing to practice flawless hospitality can tear down everything we have worked so hard to build.

> **Brown:** This is so true. Without flawless hospitality, you will lose people before you say hello.

Hospitality for us begins before Sunday morning as persons on the hospitality ministry and prayer team begin praying for members and guests who we have the audacity to believe God is going to send our way each week. We pray a prayer of blessing on their families; we pray that God will prepare their hearts and minds for worship; we pray for their protection as they drive to The Village; and we pray for their experience once they are inside the four walls. We want people to feel the power of God before they drive onto the parking lot.

Once people drive up onto the parking lot of The Village, our hospitality expands. Our Men's Ministry (Man-to-Man) has been charged to help park cars, open car doors, and then walk persons up to the worship center.

> **Brown:** Totally awesome! We didn't offer enough creative hospitality when we first started our new church.

We want persons to have a quick preview of who we are and what we stand for, which is exemplified in making persons feel at home before they step foot into the sanctuary. For example, when Mother Nature decides to open up the floodgates, we make sure that when we greet persons at their car, we have an umbrella in hand. We started our umbrella ministry following a Sunday morning downpour. I noticed that many people were running through the parking lot, others were dropping off passengers at the door, all in an attempt to avoid looking like they just came out of the shower. I thought to myself, "This is ridiculous! Why are we not outside with our umbrellas, providing hospitality to persons who braved the weather conditions to come to church?" This led me to pick up my umbrella before worship, even though I had to preach, and walk out to the parking lot to meet people at their cars and walk them to the worship center.

> **Brown:** Leaders who model service are powerful and ignite a passion of service in their congregations.

The responses and facial expressions of people when they looked out their car window and saw a smiling face standing there with an umbrella was very powerful. I knew we had provided flawless hospitality. Some of the members came up to me and told me that I should not be walking persons with an umbrella. Instead I needed to be inside preparing for worship. While preparing for worship is important, I saw an opportunity to teach on what leading by example looks like. I would never ask The Village to do something I am not willing to do myself. Setting the example led other men to pick up their umbrellas and we launched our umbrella ministry.

Flawless hospitality applies even after walking from the parking lot to the front door of the worship center. It is our goal to make sure that every person who walks through the doors feels like they are the most important person in the world.

> **Baughman:** I had the opportunity once to guest preach at The Village UMC and brought my (then) eleven-year-old daughter with me. We were the only white people in the church, but it became my daughter's favorite church of all the ones we've visited. She felt incredibly welcome there from the moment we stepped out of our car to the moment we left. The kind of intentionality behind the scenes that Derek talks about translates to a real experience for people who pull up to his church.

We live by the law that the first impression we make is the impression that will make the difference, whether it is positive or negative. Sometimes a person's decision whether or not to call a place their community is made at the door. We only get one shot. Word of mouth can either work in our favor or it can work against us and cripple the ministry. Therefore, we make sure that all persons who are on our hospitality teams, especially those posted at the doors, are passionate about people. If a person is not a people person that does not necessarily mean there is not a place for them to serve. Perhaps a person who does not like people can serve on the basement committee or the clean-up crew after everyone has left the building. But they cannot and will not serve on hospitality. It is just too important. We want persons smiling and not frowning in order to build the best possible experience.

Financial Support

Our work of sustaining new African American faith communities is a large and important task. If we are going to be successful, then a well-developed funding structure is vital to our work. Earlier I mentioned that The Village began as a daughter congregation of our mother church. I strongly believe the mother/daughter model is very effective in helping to launch and sustain new faith communities. We were able to take the DNA from our mother and implant it into another mission field ripe for kingdom building.

> **Rangel:** If we were to plant another Casa Linda somewhere else, indeed we would do it keeping the same DNA we have now. However, there should be space for contextualization. The fact that the DNA works in North East Dallas does not necessarily mean it would work in South Dallas.

We are grateful to be able to do this. It has been life changing. Without the financial support from the mother church and conference, however, the daughter church will never grow up to full maturity. When we began to vision for this ministry, a team of people put together a solid financial proposal, which was designed to cover a period of three years. The proposal was reviewed by the North Texas Annual Conference and unanimously approved. It consisted of a grant, which over the same period of time would be matched by our mother church. Our conference believed in this vision so much they awarded us the largest grant ($500,000) in the history of the North Texas Conference at that time.

Now let me be clear that being awarded a large sum of money did not mean we would automatically be successful. Money does not always lead to success. I have seen churches and corporations with plenty of money still not be effective or successful. How we use and budget the money is what makes the difference. At The Village we preached back when we launched and we continue to preach that we are called to be good stewards of everything God has entrusted us to manage. To this day, we look to spend wisely and pinch every single penny. We also believe that if we are faithful with our blessings, God will bless us with more. That is exactly what God has done and continues to do at The Village. Members and friends of The Village have seen for themselves that we are good stewards, and it has led to a consistent flow of tithes and offerings to continue supporting the vision of the ministry.

Every new church start needs an effective financial package, and without it success greatly decreases. It would not even be fair to the launch team to send them out into a mission field with insufficient funds. If we nickel-and-dime new church starts, we will end up with a nickel-and-dime ministry on life-support getting ready to pull the plug.

In my experience, African American new church starts and existing congregations can be sustainable. The Village experience has proved that there is an effective model at our fingertips that we can use for church growth. We no longer need to waste the precious breath God has given to us talking about the decline of the African American Church in United Methodism. We no longer have to talk about death, for we know that life is possible. We might need to tweak this model to fit certain contexts, but it does work. All we have to do is put the model to practice and work it.

I am excited about the future of the African American Church in United Methodism. We have enough clergy and laypersons in our connection that have the gifts, talents, drive, energy, and passion for such a time as this to reach the mission field and make disciples of Jesus Christ for the transformation of the world. Our task is not easy; it will be challenging, but who does not love a good challenge?

Brown: These are wonderful and important insights from the Village Church and Derek Jacobs that will help transform your new church and launch other new churches with confidence in yourself and God.

Size Matters

JERRY HERSHIPS, AFTERHOURS

You have heard it said . . .

Let me go on record as saying I was against the title of this chapter. Not to worry, I'm working through my issues.

But despite the humor, I think it asks an honest question: When it comes to making disciples—people who are trying to get better at living like Jesus—is having them sit in a certain room at a certain time, on a certain day, and listen to certain people, the best way? And the more the better? I'm not sure it is. If we are honest, the number of butts in the pews is the *most* important number we are often concerned with—that or the numbers on the offering sheet. We assume that worship attendees and donors equal disciples. We may be missing the mark.

Jerry Herships is the founding pastor for AfterHours in Denver, Colorado. ◆ afterhoursdenver.org

But I say to you . . .

I think the idea of worship attenders being important might be a faulty premise. On the contrary, more attenders in worship does not necessarily equal more disciples, 'cause let's not kid ourselves. The goal of many churches is not about "winning" people over to Christ, even when they say it is. Because we all know that "winning" people over to Christ means a lot more than getting them to go to church on Sunday. When it comes to the kingdom of God, I don't think God cares nearly so much about size as God cares about sacrifice and impact.

> **Ruffle:** Well said, Jerry. I think we need to liberate ourselves from the confinements that would have size and money control the trajectory of our mission. We can form new places for new people that are intimate (think the size of Jesus's group of disciples); that are a gathering of some fifty people (think community of faith); and we can try to bring together larger groups of people (think celebration group of 150 or more). Whatever the size, the faith community needs to be about bringing the hands, heart, and hope of Jesus into the community. I do think that God cares about our sacrifice and the impact we make in the communities we serve.

I think small groups can make huge impacts.

So I think there needs to be an honest moment of reflection among all of us that choose to call ourselves followers of Jesus Christ. *Why* do we want more people in the pews? Assuming we have an answer to that, we have to ask two fundamental questions: How *do* we get money? (Let's be honest. Running this show costs money.) And how do we truly make disciples, because I think we know becoming like Christ rarely happens by just listening to stories about Christ.

"Winning people over to Christ" means inviting people to do, to follow, to practice, not to "study" Christ. We *know* this. But the studying, praising, learning, and admiring is just so much *easier.*

> **Baughman:** I feel like often when someone says they want to grow in their discipleship or faith, the church sends them to a class—as if following Jesus is primarily an intellectual exercise. We assume that if we teach them something, they will live their lives differently. In my experience, getting people to change their lifestyle only happens when we challenge them to change their lifestyle.

Now none of the things listed here in this chapter are reinventing the wheel, but here are some things we have to get better at as we shift the paradigm from believer on Sunday to how those beliefs function all the days between Sundays.

We Have to Become Better Storytellers

Storytelling doesn't have to be about the "once upon a time" variety. Good stories paint pictures with words. I am so thankful that comedy helped me learn to do this. You know who doesn't generally teach storytelling? Seminaries. For institutes of higher learning, passing on knowledge is central. . . . Thinking about *how* that knowledge is passed on isn't. That's a shame. Telling a persuasive story is central to getting people engaged with your mission. People simply do not act until they are moved to act. The only way that will happen is to touch their heart.

> **Baughman:** Jerry's hitting on one of my biggest frustrations with seminaries. I believe that they train people to be lawyers because the fundamental way by which seminarians are evaluated is their ability to construct sound theological arguments. This is the work

of attorneys. Here's the thing. Nobody follows a lawyer, but they will follow a good storyteller. It might be worth noting that Jesus made fun of the lawyers and generally told stories in response to complex theological questions like the nature of the kingdom of God. By the way, most trial lawyers are trained in the art of storytelling because it's way more persuasive with a jury than arguing facts.

Nonprofits have known this for years. The church is behind—data and history have shown us this. At AfterHours we never "ask." We tell the story of how we have taken God to the streets and how they have helped us do this. The next day, online giving always shoots up. People *want* to be moved. It isn't them. It's us. When you make them fall in love with you and your story or at least with your mission through the use of story, your people can move mountains.

I know Facebook isn't exactly the Algonquin Round Table, but it has been a forum, a platform, dare I say a pulpit for sharing ideas and stories. It teaches us to use as few words as possible to convey and ignite a feeling. (I love the supposed quote of Abraham Lincoln when he said "I'm sorry my sermon is so long. If I had more time, it would have been shorter.") I cannot count the number of times people have come up to me and said how much they love my posts, especially my stories from the street and the way that God is moving in the world. They tell me it gives them concrete examples that there is still good and light in a world that is far too often painted as a place of darkness. I have almost completely given up my Facebook page as being "my" page. It belongs to AfterHours . . . except for the occasional post about bourbon, tequila, or a photo of a filet mignon I am particularly proud of. (Incidentally, we have a "page" for AfterHours. I will often copy/paste what I write on mine and put it on the AH page. It gets a tenth of the comments and traffic. People want to connect with people, not companies and institutions.)

In addition to telling an impactful story, I have also worked hard developing elevator pitches of my stories I can tell quickly. People have short attention spans, but they are thirsty for a good, uplifting story. I love the idea in storytelling of "open with a laugh, close with a tear." It is the tension between the two that makes for a memorable story. Now I am not advocating for jokes. Use humor, not jokes. George Clooney is humorous. . . . Chris Rock tells jokes. Both successful. But telling jokes is *much* harder. We are not trying to be stand-up comics. Elements of good storytelling have tension between joy and sadness. They work together. That's why the best stories have both drama and humor in them. We can, and we must, develop this skill set.

We have good news. We just have to work on getting it to them.

Praise People

Man, sometimes I think the Church is allergic to giving a compliment to people and communities. I see pastors busting their asses and getting almost no recognition for it. Now I know we didn't get in this job to get praised. We came to this job to be servants. But even servants perform better when they are told "great job."

I am not quite sure why we have an aversion to praising folks. It costs nothing, takes almost no time, and has *huge* return on investment. We are always looking for ways to make a buck go farther in the church. Here is an easy way. Shoot out a compliment. I have had bishops and DS's do this for me, and it makes me want to work just that much harder.

> **Baughman:** We've come to a similar conclusion at Union. Every time I step up to preach I first publicly celebrate two or three members of our community with the difference they are making in Union, Dallas, or their personal life. It connects us, inspires people to do more, and communicates to the congregation that I know what is happening in their lives.

I also believe the inverse is true too: If you constantly point out how people are doing it wrong, you will be able to see the result of that also in frustration, sadness, and a drop in energy and excitement for the gospel.

This doesn't just work with paid employees. I try to sing the praises of my volunteers (I hate the word *volunteer*. It just feels lame. I love leaders. Some are paid, some aren't, but my folks are leaders.) I get excited when they do a kick-ass job, and I tell them so! It's a beautiful thing to see!

I have heard people say you have to be careful with giving too much praise, because they could get a big head. I think we are so far from this being a problem it is almost laughable. Yes, there are those who will take praise and let it inflate their ego. I've been guilty of this. I get that. Having said that, we get beat up on a daily basis in our society. Let's try to be 180 degrees away from the world's way of thinking about this.

At AfterHours it is a rare day when we will have more than fifty at a worship gathering on a Monday night, but we have hundreds of volunteers who may help us in the park on any given week. They hand out food, drinks, and socks every day of the week. We get help from companies and congregations from all over the city and all walks of life. They all have responded well to being told they are living the gospel, acting like Christ, and doing a killer job of helping their community. Who wouldn't want to hear that?

So many awesome people help in a million ways.

We need to tell them.

Don't Tell People to "Bring People"

Telling people to "bring people" always feels like an act of desperation to me.

Ruffle: I get what Jerry is saying here. I do think that people will naturally tell others about experiences that are real, honest, and important to them. Hopefully we don't have to ask them. Hopefully the sharing of good news will happen spontaneously. I also know that I am the kind of introverted person that sometimes needs a push or at least an invitation to share with others what is good.

As one of the guys who was always desperately asking out the girl, I have learned that no one wants desperate or needy. When we ask people to bring people or "invite their friends," two things happen.

One, your folks can sometimes feel as though they are being used. "You just want me for my contact list." This of course isn't true, but it can come across this way. No one wants to feel like they are being played, especially by the faith leaders of their church.

The second thing is that it makes us look desperate (granted, we might be); but we don't want to *look* that way! Desperate never works. It doesn't work in relationships, it doesn't work in auditions, and it doesn't work in churches, especially new ones.

If I find a restaurant I love, I tell everyone about it. I bring them there, I introduce them to the staff, and nine times out of ten, my friends see what I love about the place. Now the owner never told me to do this. I do it because I love the place. Hell, I might *not* do it if the owner did ask me. It was of my own free will, my desire to turn friends on to this place I love that made the whole thing work. It was organic, real, legit.

One of the greatest feelings I have is when I see people I love at AfterHours bring people they love. Often it's boyfriends or girlfriends. Sometimes it's brothers or sisters. A couple of cool times it was twenty-somethings bringing their parents! That was cool.

Excitement has to be genuine. Otherwise it looks plastic, forced, and manipulative.

Don't do that.

Don't Be a Pain in the Ass

People want to work with people they enjoy working with. I learned this in Hollywood. A lot of people can do the job, whatever it is. When I was auditioning for commercials, I would walk into a waiting room for my shot to audition and *everyone* (not even kidding—every single guy) would be six feet tall, 185 pounds, with brown hair, and wearing khakis and that French blue shirt that was so popular in the early '90s. Every one of them. The job usually entailed saying *maybe* a sentence or two. Any number of people could have done the job based on talent alone. It wasn't Shakespeare. No one wanted to hear my motivation for using extra tough Hefty bags. The key almost always came down to one thing: Be someone they want to be with. If you can't be that, at least don't be a tool.

One time I was at a lecture at UCLA on the state of comedy. One of the panelists was Steve Allen, former host of *The Tonight Show.* We all got to write down a question on a 3x5 card and turn it in and there was a possibility of it being selected. Mine was one of the ones selected. When Mr. Allen asked, "Where is Jerry at?" I raised my hand and he read my question: "What does it take to be a good late night talk show host?" He looked at me completely seriously and said, "Be likable." And then he added, "And own three suits." I think that advice is useful for leaders of faith community as well.

> **Ruffle:** Reading this, I wonder if we can teach people to be likable or if that is just a gift. I like Jerry's suggestions to remember to laugh and smile and try not to be a pain. It's a start. Maybe we need a coach for this.

Find a way to connect to your people. Laugh, smile, encourage, and don't be a pain in the ass.

We have a good time when we gather at AfterHours *and* we also talk about heavy stuff. You can do both. We like to think we are throwing a party for Jesus. I mention in my book *Last Call* that "We have relegated the sacred to the somber." I think that's a shame.

Do Only Stuff You Are Excited About

I have come to realize that one of my main jobs at AfterHours is to get people excited. I'm an inspiration instigator, a holy trouble-maker. My job is to ignite ideas with excitement. Let's face it, the God business has gotten lame. It is hard to get excited about so much of what we do, *and it shouldn't be!* Jesus was a badass and his story is amazing. On top of that, people are doing the work of God every day and doing amazing things. My job has become grabbing the megaphone and turning up the volume on the gospel . . . especially in how it lives and breathes in our lives on a daily basis. We have been too calm and quiet and still for too long.

I have accidentally developed a rule. I have begun to realize over the years I am one of those people who can start a hundred projects. I am also one of those people who can easily get bored and not finish ninety of them. This has forced me to develop this rule: I simply ask myself the question, "Am I excited by this proj-ect? Do I feel my heart race at the thought of it? Does it make me smile or laugh or move me?" If all that's true, I move forward and try to get others excited about it too. If not, I ask myself more ques-tions to see if there is a way I can get excited by the idea: What am I missing? If I see that I'm not missing anything or if I can't find something to add to the idea or even get me excited, we drop it. For AfterHours, one of our rules is: Only do projects we can get excited about.

We had a huge turnout for *The Three Rev's* event that we did a few years back. (Some other clergy and I guest bartended at one of our AfterHours locations.) The bar where we held it happens to be a relatively famous dive bar in Denver. For three hours, all our tips went to the homeless and needy of the city. It was a bash! We had a great time. We packed the place and we raised hundreds of dollars for AfterHours. That was something I could get excited about.

Similarly, I was very excited about Thankful for Long Johns (when we give away underwear on Thanksgiving Day to our friends without homes), marching in the Pridefest parade, and Last Call Christmas.

Last Call Christmas is an event we've done for years at a bar which will remain nameless (mostly because of the fact I'm not entirely sure if what we did was legal). At this bar, two of my closest clergy buddies, Cindy Bates and Carolyn Waters, and I would do a short Christmas Eve service after last call on Christmas Eve (which, I guess at 1:30 in the morning, was technically Christmas Day). We would stand around the pool table, tell the Christmas story, break bread, and celebrate Communion. After we did that, we would light candles that one of us had stolen from our church earlier that evening (don't judge, man!). We would stand around the pool table and sing "Silent Night." The whole thing lasted *maybe* twenty minutes. What followed *after* that was what was even more magical.

We heard confessions.

We would sit at the bar until probably 2:30 or so, maybe or maybe not having an adult beverage, just hearing peoples' stories. What got them to a dive bar at last call on Christmas Eve? We heard stories of multiple DUIs, stories of abortions, stories of broken relationships, lost jobs, and failed attempts of getting their life together. Marcus Borg used to speak of "thin places"—places where you feel like you could almost reach out and touch the holy because in that moment the veil between heaven and earth was as thin as tissue. Sitting in this bar at a quarter to three and hearing these sacred tales of loss and shame and heartache—it was a thin place.

> **Baughman:** Offering opportunities for confession is one of the most underutilized practices in the church. I find that I can get away with asking absurdly personal questions from people because most people are dying for someone to ask. We don't like to carry our pain alone. These moments of vulnerability can lead to deep bonds of trust and support—so long as we, who have been trusted, honor the sacred nature of confession.

It isn't always so somber. One year there were three guys who happened to be in the bar dressed in long robes, beards, and birthday hats. They made it clear that they didn't want us shoving Jesus down their throats, and we promised them we wouldn't. We would just tell this story in regular words with normal terms, talking the way "normal" people talk. When we were done, one of them came over and said, "I'm still not real sure about the whole organized religion thing, but what you just did right there, that was pretty badass."

I'll take it.

We have also done nationwide events. AfterHours was not directly involved in every location, but we were the troublemakers who got the ball rolling.

One of the most successful events we have done, *PBJ for Hunger,* came out of the idea that while it is great to get praised for all these "creative ideas" AfterHours has, it's even cooler when other people who hear about what we do join in on the simple task of making peanut butter and jelly sandwiches. We found out when national PBJ day was (yes, it's an actual day), and the first Sunday after that date we asked people and groups all over the country to make PBJs, find people in need in their community, and hand them out. That was it: Make, find, give. By the end of the day, we had fed over nine thousand people all over the country. It was amazing what *got* done, just because we all agreed it *could* be done. It has been an ongoing event now for a number of years.

Probably our best event, one that could be done by any church anywhere in the country, is *Christmas in the Park*. It started with an observation: "God, it would suck to be homeless on Christmas," followed by asking a few friends the question: Why don't we try to do something about that?

People would show up, set up a card table, and start handing out whatever they thought the needy of the community could use. Its first year we had *maybe* a dozen people handing out goods and about the same amount receiving our goods. But each year over the past seven years it has grown. And grown. And grown. Last year we had over five hundred volunteers and more than seven hundred of our friends without homes show up. We had people handing out soap and toothpaste, and gloves and scarves and hats. One family had been planning this for the whole year and had been buying and saving men's underwear. They handed out 668 pairs of tighty-whities last Christmas. One group handed out tamales, one gave away oranges. One church brought an industrial-size grill and made over six hundred hamburgers.

> **Baughman:** I have found that people—whether they are involved in church or not—will rally around opportunities to serve that are innovative and/or fun. If there is a spark of creativity, crowds will attend. The more we push for innovative and fun ways to make a positive difference, the more we will be able to rally entire neighborhoods (as well as our congregants) to follow Jesus's example.

A couple of years back, AfterHours gave away more than two hundred sleeping bags, winter coats, and backpacks. This year we gave away five hundred sleeping bags and five hundred brand-new winter coats. We had a makeshift choir made up of homeless and housed alike singing carols. It was amazing. We actually celebrated the gift of giving.

An hour later, it was done.

Everything was packed up and taken away.

It was a flash mob for joy.

Keep Your Ears and Eyes Open

Look for where God is showing up. These moments where God says hello happen daily and constantly. It is what I try to do every day I'm in the park. We are not "bringing" God to the park. God is already there. We are usually just too busy to notice. The park forces me to slow down. To keep my eyes and ears open.

This is something that, no matter how many people are in our faith communities, we can train ourselves to do. This is a way to get the people in your faith community to see Christ in the world all around them 24/7 rather than just Sunday morning. You don't need a massive congregation to pull this off. When I started seeing needs in the community more, I shared what I saw. Didn't know they needed socks. We asked. They told us. Didn't think about the fact that they needed bus passes. We asked. They told us. Basic things. But we have to keep our eyes open. Next thing you know, people in the AfterHours community started seeing it as well, and sharing it. It almost looks like, dare I say it . . . evangelism. We aren't just handing out "goods"; we are seeing the last and the lost. We are looking them in the eye. We are reaching out to "the other." We are doing what we believe Jesus would do, with the people he would be doing it with. And in so doing this, modeling what Christ looks like in the world. St. Francis said, "Preach the gospel at all times. When necessary, use words." We believe that shit with our whole heart. And then people who came with us to the park started saying things like, "Hey Jerry, I work in a hotel, and we got a bunch of extra little soaps and shampoos. Could our guys use them?" and "Hey Jerry, my company had a picnic this weekend and has a ton of extra bottled water. Could you use it?" Yes please.

Now, in both these cases, the companies had had picnics before, and the hotel had had little soaps. What changed is what they saw.

They saw the opportunity to be Christ.

Measure the Impact OUTSIDE the Walls of Your Church, Not INSIDE

Bishop Mike Rhinehart is an ELCA bishop who at one time said these words about the survival of the church: "The turnaround of the mainline churches will happen when we in those churches care as much about those outside the church, as we do those inside. To embrace relevance, we will have to let go of survival."

I could not agree more. The majority of the general public couldn't care less about our choir concerts, Bible studies, and tours of the Holy Land. To be clear, these are all awesome things. They feed members of congregations and offer up opportunities to fill our time in productive ways at our church. They give people community, knowledge, and many times, joy. All good things. It's just that most people outside the church don't care.

Any success that lifts up the wider community and helps those that might not always, for one reason or another, be able to help themselves, that is going to be a success noticed by those outside the walls of the church.

The best, most impactful, most noticeable things that After-Hours has done has always been "outside" focused. Whether it is our daily lunches and Communion in the park, Last Call Christmas, PBJ for Hunger, Thankful for Long Johns, or any of the events I mentioned earlier—all of these impacted the wider community outside the church and all were great hits in a variety of ways: They cost us next to nothing to do, they got people to come into direct contact with the poor or those who don't have a particular faith community, and they were upbeat and fun! Again, joy burst through!

I believe any faith community could do any of these things, regardless of size. Because when it comes to some things—paychecks, horsepower, and French fries—size does matter. When it comes to having a positive effect on the world and building the kingdom of God and bringing heaven to earth? Goliath don't always win. Be David. And prepare to be amazed.

NOTES

Foreword: Cartographers

1. Peter Turchi, *Maps of the Imagination* (San Antonio: Trinity University Press, 2007), 11.

2. Brian Sibley and John Howe, *The Maps of Tolkien's Middle-Earth* (New York: Houghton Mifflin, 1994), 5–7; for one of many accounts of the origins of *Treasure Island*, see http://www.treasureislandthe untoldstory.com/robert-louis-stevenson.htm; http://www.cs.mcgill.ca /~rwest/link-suggestion/wpcd_2008-09_augmented/wp/t/Treasure _Island.htm.

Church Planters Have to Be Like the People They Serve

1. United States Census Bureau. "State & County QuickFacts: Dallas County," MissionInsite 7–8.

2. Viv Grigg, *Companion to the Poor: Christ in the Urban Slums* (Authentic and World Vision, 2004), 52.

Planting Churches Requires Clergy

1. Sam Hodges, "Part Time Pastors Claiming More Pulpits," *United Methodist News Services*, Sept. 28, 2015, http://www.umc.org /news-and-media/part-time-pastors-claiming-more-pulpits.

2. Ibid.

3. Alan Hirsch, *The Forgotten Ways* (Grand Rapids: Brazos Press, 2006), 20, 23, 103.

4. I arrived at this figure through interviews with several congregational development personnel in different annual conferences, as well as church plant coaches.

Truly Multiethnic Churches Don't Work

1. Christie House, Global Ministries of the United Methodist Church, *Choosing at the Crossroads: School of Congregational Development 2015*, Indianapolis, Indiana, August 16, 2015. See also Pew Research Center, *Religion and Public Life Study for 2014.*

2. Sam Rodriguez, *Intentional Multiethnic Church Planting*, a Path1 (New Church Starts) blog of the General Board of Discipleship of the United Methodist Church, http://www.umcdiscipleship.org/blog /article/intentional-multi-ethnic-church-planting.

3. Ed Stetzer, "Thinking Through the Multicultural Church," *Christianity Today*, December 3, 2013.

4. Rick Warren, *The Purpose Driven Church: Every Church Is Big in God's Eyes* (Grand Rapids: Zondervan, 1995), 176.

5. *"Racial Attitudes of Blacks in Multiracial Congregations Resemble Those of Whites, Study Finds,"* Press Release by @BaylorUMedia Aug. 17, 2015, for a national study done by researchers at Baylor University, the University of Southern California, and the University of Chicago. The actual study, *"United by Faith? Race/Ethnicity, Congregational Diversity, and Explanations of Racial Inequality"* is published in the journal *Sociology of Religion.*

6. Ibid.

7. Lisa Asedillo Cunningham, *Mixed Race Perspective: Boundary Crossing Ethics and the Thunder Perfect Mind*, masters of divinity thesis, Union Theological Seminary, May 2015.

8. Donnie McClurkin, *Days of Elijah*, Songs, Hymns, and Spiritual Songs, 2004.

9. Caroline Bankoff, "Ramarley Graham's Family Receives $3.9 Million Settlement," *New York Magazine*, January 31, 2015, http:// nymag.com/daily/intelligencer/2015/01/grahams-family-gets-39 -million-settlement.html.

CPSIA information can be obtained
at www.ICGtesting.com
Printed in the USA
FSOW03n1628210617
35502FS